Munich

Colored engraving (ca. 1740). View of Marienplatz.

Guide to the most beautiful sights

Text by Andreas Kegel and Astrid Güldner, Munich

Kunstverlag Edm. von König, Heidelberg/Dielheim

"Grüss Gott" in Munich

Although Munich is a bustling international city, it is affectionately regarded by some of its citizens as the largest village in Germany.

Surveys have shown that the capital of the state of Bavaria is the best-loved of all German cities and the one where many Germans would most like to live.

Every year, Munich plays host to more than 3 million tourists from all over the world.

What is it that makes this city – incidentally, one of the most expensive in Germany – so fascinating?

One factor is certainly the excellent leisure opportunities that it offers: for example, sunbathing on the banks of the Isar followed by a relaxing visit to a beer garden, sailing or windsurfing on the Ammersee, and the broad spectrum its cultural life, including important museums, theaters and festivals. Also, it's just an hour's drive to the mountains, while Lake Garda in northern Italy is only six hours away.

Munich is an important center of higher education, banking, and the film and media industry. The venue of many international trade fairs and congresses, the city contains the headquarters of many multinational companies (Siemens, BMW, MAN, MTU). Of course, it is also the home of world-famous beers.

And what about the city's inhabitants, the "Münchners"?

The increasing number of visitors to Munich has helped to dispel the old clichés of men sporting leather shorts and tufted hats grumbling into their beer mugs and accompanied by generously proportioned blond Fräuleins. Nonetheless, there are certain traits that could be called typically Bavarian: a certain "rough" warmth and friendliness, the relaxed atmosphere of the beer garden, the feeling of "live and let live": these are still things that help make the city so attractive and memorable for its visitors.

The Bavarian capital is located on the Swabian-Bavarian plateau and is surrounded by the valleys of the Ammersee and Lake Starnberg. The city owes its existence primarily to its site on the River Isar, which traverses it from the south east to the north east.

The highest point of the city is the Warnberg (578 meters above sea level), while the fields leading down to the Isar in the north west of the city are the lowest point (478 meters above sea level). To the north of Munich are located the Dachau and Erdinger Moors.

For those who like to know things exactly, the city center (Cathedral Church of Our Lady) lies at a latitude of 48°8'23" north and a longitude of 11°34'28" east. The city and its suburbs comprise a total area of over 30,000 hectares.

With a population of about 1.3 million, Munich is the third-largest city in Germany. It is the capital of the Free State of Bavaria as well as of the region of Upper Bavaria. Munich is the seat of the government, parliament and Supreme Court of Bavaria. The government of the city is in the hands of the directly elected Lord Mayor and two deputy mayors chosen from the ranks of the city council and experts on administrative matters.

Munich lies on the border between the maritime west European and continental east European climate zones, and its weather is also influenced by the nearby Alpine chain. An unusual feature of the Munich climate is the so-called

View from the city center toward the north (in the foreground, the tower of the New City Hall)

föhn, a dry, warm fall wind that originates in the Alps and can occur at any time of year.

The föhn brings not only a strikingly clear view but is also often blamed (not always fairly) for headaches, bad moods and lack of concentration ("you see, it's the föhn's fault" is a favorite excuse).

Our city guide begins with a round tour through the Old City, while chapters 2–8 deal with the important sights in other parts of the city. These areas are presented in a sequence and form that allows each to be covered as an individual sight-seeing tour. The numbers in brackets refer to the numbered places indicated on the accompanying map. Let's begin, though, with a brief summary of the history of the city.

Key Dates and Events in the History of Munich

10/11th century	On the banks of the Isar, monks from Tegernsee Abbey establish a settlement called "Munichen" (the name derives from the German word for monks, "Mönche"). The municipal coat-of-arms recalls the city's monastic origins.
1158	Founding of the city by the Guelph, Henry the Lion. This duke destroys the Bishop of Freising's toll bridge over the Isar and establishes a town market and mint. First city fortification.
1180	After the expulsion of Henry the Lion, Bavaria becomes part of the territory controlled by the Wittelsbachs.
1255	Munich becomes the main residence of the Wittelsbachs.
1314–47	Reign of Ludwig IV ("the Bavarian"), who is made Holy Roman Emperor in 1328. Munich becomes the imperial capital and, in 1340, is granted city privileges. Construction of the second defensive ring wall.
1467–1508	Under the rule of Albrecht IV (called "the Wise"), the city enjoys a high point in Gothic culture with artists such as Grasser and Polack.
1505	Munich becomes the capital of united Bavaria.
1550–79	Duke Albrecht V supports the Counter Reformation. Building of the Antiquarium in the Residence.
1609	Setting up of the Catholic League.
1618–48	Thirty Years War.
1632	Occupation of Munich by Gustavus Adolphus of Sweden.
1634	The plague results in 7000 deaths – one-third of the city's population.
1651–79	Under Elector Ferdinand Maria, start of the construction of the Theatiner Church.
1679–1726	Prince Elector Max II Emanuel. After triumphs over the Turks, a change of political fortunes leads to the occupation of Munich by Austrian troops in 1705–14 as a consequence of the War of Spanish Succession. A peasant rising against the occupation forces is brutally suppressed ("Sendlinger Christmas Massacre" with the famous figure, the "Smith of Kochel"). During this Elector's reign, extension of Nymphenburg Castle and Schleissheim Castle.
1777–99	Prince Elector Karl Theodor. Union of Bavaria and the Palatinate (Pfalz).
1799–1825	Prince Elector Max IV Joseph (after 1806, King Max I).
1800	Occupation by French troops of the Revolutionary Army.
1806	Bavaria becomes a kingdom.
1810	A horse race on the occasion of the wedding of the Crown Prince begins the tradition of the Oktoberfest.
1818	Bavaria receives its first constitution.
1825–48	Under Ludwig I, Munich becomes the "Athens on the Isar." Extension of the Residence, construction of Ludwigstrasse and Königsplatz.

The monk in the city's coat-of-arms recalls the first monastic settlement of "Mönchen"

1826	Munich becomes a university city.
1846	Munich's population reaches 100,000.
1848	The "March Uprising" leads to political unrest throughout Germany. First German parliament meets in the Paulskirche in Frankfurt.
1848–64	King Max II.
1864–86	Reign of the "Fairy Tale" King, Ludwig II.
1886–1912	"Prince Regency" under Luitpold.
1918	November Revolution under the leadership of Kurt Eisner. Flight of King Ludwig III and proclamation of the Free State of Bavaria.
1919	The communist soviet republic (Räterepublik) is brutally crushed by troops of the Reichswehr.
1923	Failure of Hitler's Beer Hall Putsch.
1933	Construction of the concentration camp in Dachau.
1939	Abortive attempt by Georg Elsner to assassinate Hitler in the Bürgerbräukeller.
1943	Execution of the Scholls, the leaders of the resistance group, the "White Rose."
1945	After the Second World War, the city is a scene of devastation, with nearly half of its buildings destroyed. A remarkable rebuilding effort (nicknamed "Rama Dama") begins under Mayor Thomas Wimmer. Not only are almost all of the city's historic buildings rebuilt, but many new suburbs are added.
1946	New Bavarian constitution. Munich becomes the capital of the Free State of Bavaria.

1957	Munich's population reaches 1 million.
1966–72	Construction of the city's subway and streetcar network.
1972	The 20th Summer Olympic Games are held in Munich. Arabian terrorists hold members of the Israeli team hostage in the Olympic village. The rescue attempt ends with bloodshed and tragedy.
1980	A bomb attack during the Oktoberfest claims 12 lives.
1981	Opening of the Neue Pinakothek.
1985	Opening of the Gasteig Arts Center.
1992	World Economic Summit Meeting in Munich. Opening of the Franz Josef Strauss Airport.
1993	Completion of the Bavarian State Chancellery buildings.

Walking Tour of the Old City

Munich offers so many interesting sights that it is best to approach it in stages rather than trying to do everything "in one go."

To help you get the most out of the city, this guide is arranged so that it deals in detail with the various historical and cultural aspects of the Old City (Altstadt) within the context of a 6- to 8-hour round trip.

Marienplatz traditionally marks the center of the city

Marienplatz and the Church of St. Peter

Marienplatz (1) has been regarded as the center of Munich ever since the founding of the city by Henry the Lion in 1158.

Until early in the nineteenth century, this square (formerly called Schrannen-platz) was the site of a grain market as well as a general agricultural market. In the Middle Ages, it was the scene of jousting tournaments, a function still re-called in the carillon of the clock on the tower of the New City Hall.

Marienplatz owes its name to the **Mary Column (Mariensäule)**, a work by Hubert Gerhard that was erected in the middle of the square in 1638. It was meant as a token of thanks to Mary, patron saint of Bavaria, for the sparing of Munich and Landshut during the occupation by Swedish troops. On the pedes-tal of the statue (which was originally intended for the Cathedral Church of Our Lady), there are four winged children that represent innocent hostages of plague, war, famine and heresy.

The square is dominated by the **New City Hall (Neues Rathaus) (2)** commis-sioned by King Ludwig I, whose construction necessitated the demolition of 24 historic houses. This neo-Gothic building (brick with carved stone ornament, the west section with tower made of muschelkalk) was erected in three phases

The Cathedral Church of Our Lady and the New City Hall

The neo-Gothic courtyard of the New City Hall

*The Mary Column,
erected in honor of the patron
saint of Bavaria*

between 1867 and 1909 under the supervision of Georg Hauberisser. Its most striking feature is the 85-meter-high tower with the famous Munich **carillon (Glockenspiel)**. Every day at 11 a.m. (from May through October, also 12 a.m., 5 p.m. and 9 p.m), 32 almost life-size figures present scenes from the city's history: the wedding of Duke Wilhelm V and Renata of Lorraine with jousting tournament, and the Coopers' Dance (Schefflertanz) that has been performed every 7 years since 1517 to celebrate the end of the Black Death. In the evening (9:30 p.m. in summer, 7:30 p.m. in winter), a night watchman and angel of peace emerge to bless the small figure of a monk (Münchner Kindl – a symbol of the city).

The carillon on the tower of the New City Hall

The facade of the New City Hall is about 100 meters long and its rich ornamentation includes figures of Bavarian dukes, princes and kings, as well as allegorical and legendary figures, and saints.

The building's courtyards with their stair turrets, staircases and spacious enclosed stairways, are modeled on Gothic castle courtyards.

Dating from 1862–65 and the work of Konrad Krull, the **Fish Fountain (Fischbrunnen)** is a favorite meeting place of young people. Until the beginning of the present century, this was where new butcher's apprentices had to undergo the traditional ceremony of the "Butcher's Leap" (Metzgersprung).

The boundary of the very first medieval city ran where the **Old City Hall (Alte Rathaus) (3)** was built by Jörg von Halspach (called Ganghofer) in 1470–80. Most of the building was destroyed in the Second World War. Located over the gateway, the Rathaussaal has beautifully ornamented timber barrel vaulting, which is a masterpiece of German late-Gothic architecture. This was the original home of the Maruska dancers – 16 wood figures carved by Erasmus Grasser in 1480 – of which, unfortunately, only 10 have been preserved (on show in the City Museum). A **toy museum (Spielzeugmuseum)** is now housed in the Rathaus tower, which was rebuilt in 1975.

View from Marienplatz toward the Old City Hall

A teddy–bear made by Steiff in 1907 in the Toy Museum

South of Marienplatz is the **church of St Peter (4),** the first and oldest parish church in the city. The 91–metre high tower, nicknamed "Old Peter", is one of the landmarks of Munich. (Visitors can climb to the top.)

The 12th–century Romanesque pillared basilica was rebuilt in the 13th century, but this was a victim of the fire that swept the city in 1327. Only the lower storeys of the west towers escaped, and were integrated into the Gothic–style building that arose alongside them (consecrated in 1368). The west part, with its taller central tower, was built between 1379 and 1386, but was not given its characteristic lantern dome until the 17th century.

The choir was also altered in the 17th century. Under the supervision of Isaak Pader, the Gothic long choir was replaced between 1630 and 1636 by a triple–conch choir, the exterior of which consists of plain, unplastered brickwork. It is intended as a reference to the Papal church of St Peter's in Rome, because Munich always harboured the ambition of becoming the "Rome of Germany".

The interior of the church is also dominated by the early Baroque choir, the big windows of which draw the eye with their floods of light. The nave was redesigned later (1730–56) with great care, and adds further to this effect by carrying over the fenestration of the choir into its wall design. The plasterwork and frescoes are the work of J.B. Zimmermann (1753–56). Much of the church was destroyed in the second world war, but most of it was reconstructed between 1946 and 1954.

The high altar (1730) includes a figure of St Peter by Erasmus Grasser (1493–95) and statues of the four Church Fathers by Egid Q. Asam (1732–33).

On the side walls of the presbytery there are five late Gothic panels by Jan Polacks (1517), once part of the High Altar.

The altar, consecrated in 1407, is a masterpiece of Gothic art showing a Christ Pantocrator and a Last Judgement. The Aresing epitaph by Erasmus Grasser (1482) is also well worth seeing.

The tower of St. Peter's is open to visitors. The ascent of about 300 steps is rewarded by a marvelous view of the city.
Open Mon.–Sat. 9 a. m. to 6 p. m.;
Sun. and Public Holidays 10 a. m. to 6 p. m.

◄ *High altar of the Church of St. Peter*   *View of Theatinerstrasse* ▼

From the Viktualienmarkt to the Isar Gate

At the foot of hill leading up to St. Peter's, one comes to the **Viktualienmarkt (5)**, a bustling market with colorful stands and stalls. This food market in the heart of the city has a long tradition going back to the beginning of the nineteenth century. Even today, its lively atmosphere owes much to the market women, whose friendliness can easily give way to decidedly earthy comments in broad Bavarian dialect when an awkward customer strains their patience.

In summer, it is particularly pleasant to enjoy the market scene from the beer garden that is set up around the maypole.

If you should happen to be in Munich on Shrove Tuesday (Faschingsdienstag), don't miss the opportunity to see the remarkable "Dance of the Market Women."

The statues on the fountain of the Viktualienmarkt recall several popular folk singers and actors associated with Munich: Karl Valentin, Liesl Karlstadt, Weiss Ferdl, Roider Jakl, Elise Aulinger and Ida Schumacher.

*Karl Valentin
Fontain on the
Viktualienmarkt*

Viktualienmarkt with the towers of the New City Hall and the Churches of St. Peter and Our Lady

At the north end of the market, we come to the **Church of the Holy Spirit (Hei-liggeistkirche) (6)**. Originally a fourteenth-century Gothic hall church belonging to the Hospital of the Holy Spirit, this was greatly altered in the Baroque style by Johann Georg Ettenhofer in 1724–30 and was refurbished by E. Q. and C. D. Asam. After the demolition of the hospital buildings, the nave was lengthened and given a neo-Baroque facade by Franz Löwel in 1885. The tower has a lantern dome, which is such a characteristic feature of Munich's churches.

Although it was seriously damaged in the war, the form and furnishings of the church have been almost entirely restored.

The Church of the Holy Spirit to the north of the Viktualienmarkt

The interior of the Church of the Holy Spirit consists of a nave with two aisles and an ambulatory encircling the chancel. The main nave has a pointed barrel vault, while the aisles have ribbed vaults. The only remaining traces of the original Gothic interior are the buttresses of the chancel and the wall along the north side of the church.

The high altar is a work by Nikolaus Stuber dating from 1730, and it contains a painting by Ulrich Loth, "The Outpouring of the Holy Spirit" (1644). The two flanking angels stem from the workshop of Johann Georg Greiff (1730). The south aisle contains a series of wall paintings by Peter Jakob Horeman called "The Seven Gifts of the Holy Spirit" (1725). In the north aisle, the figure in the altar dedicated to Mary, the so-called Hammerthal Mother of God, is an especially outstanding work dating back to about 1450. The bronze tomb of Duke Ferdinand of Bavaria from the early seventeenth century (Hans Krumpner, 1608) is to be found against the west wall.

The **Isar Gate (Isartor) (7)** was the eastern boundary of the city fortifications at the time of Ludwig the Bavarian in the fourteenth century. It is the only gate of the city whose tower has survived. The wall-painting, "The Triumphal Entry of Emperor Ludwig of Bavaria after the Battle of Ampfingen in 1322," is a work of the nineteenth century.

The south tower contains the **Valentin-Musäum**, which is dedicated to Karl Valentin (1882–1948), a sort of German Charlie Chaplin. The exhibition includes various pictures, oddities and amusing "artworks" by Valentin with titles like "Bowel Movement Sculpturally Represented" and "Sculpture of Melted Snow." Having enjoyed this most unusual museum, it's no bad idea to drop into the café, the "Valentinsmusäumsstübl."

The opening hours of the Valentin-Musäum are as odd as its contents:
Mon., Tues., Fri. and Sat. 11:01 a.m. to 5:29 p.m.; Sun. 10:01 a.m. to 5:29 p.m. The entry fee is also an "odd" amount.

The Isar Gate – a part of the city's fourteenth-century defensive wall

From the City Museum to Karlsplatz

Proceeding along Westenriedstrasse and past the Viktualienmarkt, we come to the **City Museum (Münchner Stadtmuseum) (8)** located on St.-Jakobs-Platz.

The museum's permanent collection as well as special exhibitions provide insights into the history and culture of Munich.

The museum is housed in several buildings: the former arsenal with its gabled house and corner tower (fifteenth century), the former stables (fifteenth century; rebuilt in 1978) and a twentieth-century wing annex.

The City Museum has many interesting collections on display, including historic weapons, a scale model of the city as it was in 1570, sculpture, arts and crafts, coins from the fifteenth to the twentieth century, toys, graphic arts and musical instruments, along with a particularly attractive collection relating to domestic culture in Munich, especially in the Biedermeier and Art Nouveau (Jugendstil) periods.

The Gothic Hall contains the 10 surviving Maruska dancers by Erasmus Grasser, which originally stood in the Old City Hall. These wooden figures carved in 1480 are superb examples of secular art from the Gothic period. The subject matter of the Maruska dance originates from Moorish Spain and refers to a competition of costumed singers to win the favors of a beautiful maiden.

The City Museum also contains a Photography and Film Museum with a changing program of events, as well as a very "in" café with a beer garden.

Opening hours of the City Museum (collections):
Tues. through Sun. 10 a.m. to 5 p.m.;
Weds. 10 a.m. to 8:30 p.m.

Just behind the City Museum in the Rindermarkt, we come to the **Lion Tower (Löwenturm)**, a water tower built in about 1600. Of particular interest are the **Ruffini Houses (9)** (Rindermarkt 10), which were designed as offices and business premises by Gabriel von Seidl. Built at the beginning of the present century, the most striking features of these buildings are the ornamental stucco work and the colorful facades. The **Rindermarkt Fountain** is a popular place for taking a break during a stroll through the city.

Amid the shops of the lively Sendlinger Strasse, we come upon the **Asamkirche (Church of St. John Nepomuk)** and the **Asamhaus (10)**. The Rococo church complete with vicarage and house was erected as a private chapel by the brothers, E. Q. and C. D. Asam.

As only the east wall was able to serve as a major source of light for the interior, the large wall openings are the dominant elements of the facade.

A wrought-iron screen separates the oval narthex with its carved confessionals and stucco saints from the long main body of the church, which has an encircling gallery and walls articulated by a projecting molded cornice. The impressive ceiling fresco, "The Life of St. John Nepomuk," is the work of C. D. Asam.

Surrounded by four twisted columns, the high altar contains a tabernacle with gilded stucco representing the sun and a wax figure of St. John Nepomuk (with inserted reliquary). The high altar is completed by a group of figures representing the "Seat of Mercy": God holds up to the eyes of mankind the Son of Man who died that they might be saved.

On either side of the high altar in side niches are statues of the two other saints to whom the church is dedicated: John the Baptist and St. John the Evangelist. The crypt, which is only open on special feast days (e. g., Good Friday), contains a valuable "Mother of Sorrows."

Interior of the Asamkirche: a jewel of Rococo architecture

The **Sendlinger Gate (Sendlinger Tor) (11)**, which was first mentioned in 1318, was constructed at the time when the city was expanded by Ludwig the Bavarian. The two flanking towers dating from about 1420 are the only surviving remnants of the original group of fortifications that comprised the gateway.

View toward the Sendlinger Gate

Leaving the Sendlinger Gate along Kreuzstrasse, we come to Damenstiftstrasse, which contains several buildings well worth seeing. The **Collegiate Church of St. Anne (Damenstiftskirche St. Anna) (12)** was built by Johann Baptist Gunetzrhainer in 1732–35 as the church for the Collegiate Nunnery of St. Anne. Only the outside walls and facade survived the war, and the church was rebuilt in the 1950s. The Baroque facade with its broad central portal and high clerestory windows is vertically articulated by pilasters on high columns.

The interior is distinguished by the combination of several interesting individual features: entrance bay with gallery, domed main nave and domed chancel.

The furnishings and decoration are the work of E. Q. and C. D. Asam, while the altar painting showing St. Anne, St. Mary and Jesus is by Joseph Ruffini.

Other attractive buildings in Damenstiftstrasse include a house (no. 4) in the classical style dating from about 1800 and the **Palais Lerchenfeld (13)**, a Rococo palace built by Gunetzrhainer at the beginning of the eighteenth century.

Following Herzogspitalstrasse and Sonnenstrasse, we come to **Karlsplatz (14)**, which is popularly called the "Stachus." This square was laid out in 1791 after the demolition of the city fortifications by the **Karlstor (Karl's Gate)**. Along with the Old City ring road (Altstadtring), this is the most traffic-congested place in Munich. In the 1960s, Karlsplatz became an important intersection for the city's subway (U-Bahn) and streetcar (S-Bahn) systems, with many new shops being built over an extensive underground parking lot. The semi-circular construction with neo-Baroque offices and business premises was designed by Gabriel von Seidl in about 1900.

The Karlstor (formerly the Neuhauser Tor) was rebuilt in 1861. Between 1319 and 1791, this gateway served as the entrance to the Old City through the second fortified ring wall.

Opposite Karlsplatz stands the imposing **Palace of Justice (Justizpalast) (15)**, a monumental example of late nineteenth-century architecture, which its designer, Friedrich von Thiersch, modeled on the Italian style of the late Renaissance. Its most striking feature is the polygonal dome made of iron and glass over the cental air well, a construction without precedent at the time.

Karlsplatz with its fountains and neo-Baroque buildings

*Karl's Gate: the
entrance to the Old City* ▶

◀ *The monumental
Palace of Justice*

To the north of the Palace of Justice, we come to the **Old Botanical Garden (Alter Botanischer Garten) (16)**, which was the municipal botanical garden until 1909. The entrance gateway was designed by Joseph Emanuel Herigoyen and bears a Latin dedication written by Goethe for King Max I Joseph. The garden is a popular haven for those looking for a break from the bustle of the city.

The **Artist's House (Künstlerhaus) (17)** situated on Lenbachplatz was originally conceived by Gabriel von Siedl in 1892–1900 as a meeting place for a group of established Munich artists. Its square main hall is contained within a tall

Bird's-eye view of Karlsplatz

building with curved gables, and the courtyard is enclosed by two wings. Unfortunately, only some of the original furnishings and decoration – mostly the work of Lenbach – have been preserved.

The Artist's House now contains a restaurant and a small theater.

On the east side of Lenbachplatz, we find the **Wittelsbach Fountain (Wittelsbacher Brunnen)**, a neo-classical work by the sculptor, Adolf von Hildebrandt. The statues of a youth on horseback hurling a rock and a woman with a bowl seated on a bull represent the power of and blessings brought by the element, water.

The Wittelsbach Fountain on Lenbachplatz

Pedestrian Precinct, Cathedral Church of Our Lady and Former "Noble" Quarter

Passing through the Karlstor, we come back to the **pedestrian precinct (Fuss-gängerzone)**. The area between Karlsplatz and Marienplatz has been closed to traffic since 1972. Along with Neuhauser and Kaufinger Strasse, this is one of the most important shopping areas in the city. In this "shopping mile," there are any number of department stores, restaurants, bars and boutiques, and count-less buskers and street artists offer all manner of entertainment to passersby. The pedestrian precinct also includes Frauenplatz by the Cathedral Church of Our Lady, as well as the Viktualienmarkt and the rather exclusive Theatiners-trasse, which extends from the New City Hall to Odeonsplatz.

Passing the **Brunnenbüberl (Fountain Boy)** near the Karlstor, we come to the **Bürgersaal (18)** (assembly hall for men of the Marian confraternity), which was built in 1709/10 according to plans drawn up by G. A. Viscardi. Used since 1778 as a church, this building was severely damaged in the war and rebuilt in 1946.

Apart from the side doors that were inserted later, the facade with its Tuscan double pilasters is original. The crypt contains the tomb of Father Rupert Mayer (1876–1945), whose opposition to the Nazis was to cost him his life.

The interior of the assembly hall in the upper storey (1710) is well worth seeing, with its ornamental stucco ceiling by P. F. Appiani and stucco wall decoration by J. G. Bader. The guardian angel leading a child located under the organ console is the work of Ignaz Günther (1763).

The "Fountain Boy"
(Brunnenbüberl)
by Karl's Gate

Street entertainment in the pedestrian precinct

The **Old Academy (Alte Akademie) (19)** in Neuhauser Strasse was built as a Jesuit College and High School (Gymnasium) in 1585–97. After the expulsion of the Jesuits, this Renaissance building with four courtyards was put to various uses, including housing the Academy of Fine Art and the University. The Old Academy now contains the headquarters of the Regional Statistics Office.

The history of the building of the **Church of St. Michael (20)** is closely linked with the reign of Wilhelm V "the Pious." In the wake of the Counter Reformation, he gave permission to the Jesuits to build this church, which became one of the most important Renaissance ecclesiastical buildings north of the Alps. However, the building costs almost drove the state into bankruptcy. Its construction, which began in 1583, had to be interrupted in 1590 when a tower collapsed, so that its consecration only took place in 1597.

Almost completely destroyed in the war, St. Michael's was rebuilt in 1947–48.

Facade of the "Jesuit Church" of St. Michael

Powerful horizontal elements divide the facade into three distinct tiers surmounted by a steep gable, the overall effect being reminiscent of certain medieval town halls to be found in Germany. The marble entrance portal is presided over by a bronze statue of the Archangel Michael doing battle with the evils of the world, a work of Hubert Gerhard dating from 1588. The niches contain stone statues of some of the Wittelsbach Prince Electors.

The imposing nave and long chancel comprise the first monumental Renaissance interior to be built north of the Alps, the dimensions actually exceeding those of the Il Gesù Church in Rome (da Vignola, 1568) on which it was modeled. The dominant feature is the triumphal arch of the chancel, whose form is echoed in the arches of the transepts, side chapels and galleries. Its triumphal character is meant to symbolize the victory of the Counter Reformation.

The soaring, three-storied high altar (1586–89) by Friedrich Sustris and Wendel Dietrich contains a painting showing "St. Michael Fighting the Devil" by Christoph Schwarz (1587). The four bronze reliefs by Hubert Gerhard (about 1595) were intended for the tomb of Wilhelm V, a project that was never completed. The side chapels contain fine paintings by Antonio Viviani, Hans von Aachen and Peter Candid. On the north side, there is a valuable reliquary shrine of Saints Cosmos and Damian (about 1400).

The crypt beneath the chancel is the burial place of many members of the Wittelsbach family, including Duke Wilhelm V, the Elector Maximilian and the "Fairy Tale" King, Ludwig II.

The **German Hunting and Fishing Museum (Deutsches Jagd- und Fischereimuseum) (21)** has been established in the former Augustinerkirche since 1966.

Begun in 1291, this monastery church was, for a time, the most important Gothic building in Munich. Early in the seventeenth century, it underwent considerable Baroque alterations and, after being secularized, was put to other uses.

The museum contains 500 stuffed animals exhibited in dioramas, as well as hunting weapons and equipment, hunting paintings, a large section devoted to the art of fishing and a collection of "Wolperdingen" (mythical and fantastic figures).

> **The German Hunting and Fishing Museum is open daily from 9:30 a. m. to 5 p. m. (Mon. and Thurs. until 9 p. m.).**

Entrance of the German Hunting and Fishing Museum

North of the Hunting and Fishing Museum is Munich's best–known landmarks, the **Cathedral Church of Our Lady,** also known as the **Frauenkirche (22)**. It has been the Metropolitan Church of the newly founded Archbishopric of Munich–Freising since 1821, and the turbulent history on which it can look back is closely bound up with that of the Wittelsbach monarchs and their desire for a fitting sepulchre.

A major building dating from the first half of the 13th century preceded this one, on which work started in 1468. Jörg von Halspach was commissioned to build it; he constructed the enormous church (109 metres long, 40 metres wide) in the shortest possible time, using a brick construction. The foundation stone was laid in 1468 by Duke Sigismund and Bishop Johannes Tulbeck, and the church was ceremoniously consecrated in 1494, although the "onion domes" on the two towers were not added until 1525. The three–nave Frauenkirche with its irregular polygonal choir keeps totally to the tradition of southern German wide–span churches. The clear structure of the body of the church and its massive roof is dictated by the integration of the chapel crown and the decision to dispense with a crossing.

The plain and simple external architecture is in harmony with the disciplined interior. The unyielding central nave leads directly along underneath the star vaulting to the choir window. This is all the more effective because of the tight arrangement of the octagonal pillars which, although they are tellingly modelled by the light falling on them from the side, prevent the windows themselves from being seen.

The rich interior decoration, which was constantly being altered to meet changes in artistic taste, dates from a number of different epochs, although much of it was sacrificed to the religious movements of the 19th century or to the ravages of the last war. The last phase of restoration was taken as an opportunity to bring home various important works of art such as the statues from the choir stool by Erasmus Grasser (1502); it is to him that the automatic clock alongside the Chapel of the Sacrament is ascribed. This is the oldest mechanical picture still extant, and above the clock face there are moving figures of the Virgin Mary, Christ, and God the Father (about 1500).

The three outstanding sculptures in the Chapel of the Court Brotherhood of St Anna and St George are also worthy of mention. They stand on the left of the Chapel, and represent the two patron saints of the Order – St Rasso (by the master–craftsman von Rabenden, about 1515) and St George (by Hans Leinberger, also about 1515) – and St Christopher (also by Hans Leinberger, about 1520–25). The 17th–century decoration work includes the monumental High Altar by the Court painter Peter Candid (1620), the main panel of which hangs above the sacristy door and represents the Ascension of the Virgin. The cenotaph made of bronze and black marble (1622) commemorates the Emperor Ludwig the Bavarian and includes a red marble memorial tablet of much earlier date (1490). This massive structure by Hans Krumper, with figures by Hubert Gerhard and others, used to be set up longitudinally in the choir, but is now to be found in front of the southern tower chapel. The Rococo age endowed the interior with the gilded bas–reliefs (1774) which Ignaz Günther created for the choir stool. Roman Anton Boos produced a pulpit, of which the statue of the Virgin Mary (1780) is still preserved; it originally stood atop the pulpit canopy, but now stands on a pillar in the choir.

The Cathedral Church of Our Lady: the symbol of the city

Tomb of Emperor Ludwig "the Bavarian"

Crossing the Löwengrube, we come to the **Gunetzrhainer House (23)** (Promenadeplatz 15), a lovely Rococo town house built by the court architect Gunetzrhainer in 1730. Promenadeplatz also contains the **Palais Montgelas (24)** – now the Bayerischer Hof Hotel – a palace in the classical style built in 1810 for Count Montgelas by Herigoyen.

Both of these buildings were part of the former "noble" quarter between Promenadeplatz and the Residence that came into being during the Age of Absolutism. Other splendid buildings of this quarter include the Palais Preysing, the Palais Holnstein (Archbishop's Palace) and the Palais Törring (formerly the Main Post Office), which we will come to during the course of this tour.

To the west of Promenadeplatz, we come to the **Church of the Holy Trinity (Dreifaltigkeitskirche) (25)**, which was built in 1711–18. During the War of Spanish Succession, the daughter of a citizen called Lindtmayer prophesied that Divine Judgement was about to strike Munich. To avert this, the nobility, churchmen and wealthy citizens took 1704 an oath to build a church in honor of the Holy Trinity.

The late-Baroque facade based on plans by Viscardi has a convex form and is the first of this type to be built in Bavaria.

The interior comprises a square main section and four transepts, with an extended chancel to the north. The reredos of the high altar (1716/17) is the work of Wolff and Degler and was donated by the Elector. Its subject matter recalls the oath that led to the building of the church.

The **Siemens Museum (26)**, which lies to the north of the Church of the Holy Trinity in Prannerstrasse, was founded in 1954 and documents the 140-year history of this company, which is now a multi-national concern. The museum traces the development of electrotechnology from its beginnings in the last century via electronics to microelectronics. Almost all of the objects on show are "hands

The Siemens Museum: an automobile dating from 1925

on," and the visitor is able to experience their wide range of applications. Operating models, explanatory diagrams, photos and videos provide more detailed information, especially concerning the practical applications of the technology. A multivisual display provides interesting insights into the many fields of work, the innovations and the international significance of the company.

Opening hours of the Siemens Museum:
Mon.-Fri. 9 a. m. to 5 p. m.;
Sun. 10 a. m. to 5 p. m.
Sat. and Public Holidays closed.

Our tour continues along Prannerstrasse to the **Archbishop's Palace (Erzbischöfliches Palais) (27)** located in Kardinal-Faulhauber-Strasse (no. 7). The only aristocratic palace in Munich to have been preserved in its entirety, it was built in 1733–37 by Cuvilliés the Elder for Count Holnstein. The Rococo facade, which has nine sections and a central porch, is beautifully decorated with stucco work.

Proceeding northward along Kardinal-Faulhaber-Strasse, we arrive at Briennerstrasse and **Wittelsbacher Platz (28)**, whose splendid palaces in the classical style (Palais Arco, Wittelsbach Palais) were built by Leo von Klenze between 1820 and 1825. The middle of the square is dominated by an equestrian statue of Elector Maximilian I, a classical work by Thorwaldsen (1830).

Wittelsbacher Platz with the equestrian statue of Elector Maximilian I

From here, it's only a few paces to **Odeonsplatz**, the starting point of the city's first two monumental avenues of the nineteenth century, Briennerstrasse and Ludwigstrasse. The strict classicism of its buildings (1816–28) stems from Leo von Klenze.

One part of this massive construction program is the **Palais Leuchtenberg (29)** built in 1820, which is largely based on the Palazzo Farnese in Rome. Since 1966, this classical palace has served as the headquarters of the Bavarian Ministry of Finance.

Ludwigstrasse leads to the **Commander's Hall (Feldherrnhalle) (30)**, a 20-meter-high open arcade modeled on the Loggia dei Lanzi in Florence. It was built between 1841 and 1844 by Friedrich von Gärtner on the commission of Ludwig I. The two bronze monuments honor the Bavarian military commanders, Tilly and Wrede, while the Memorial to the Bavarian Army was erected after the Franco-Prussian War of 1870/71.

The **Palais Preysing (31)** located to the south of the Commander's Hall is the first Rococo palace to have been built in Munich; it was constructed for Count Maximilian von Preysing by Joseph Effner in 1723–28. A beautiful feature of the interior of the palace – now a shopping mall – that has been preserved is the splendid triple staircase with wall decoration.

The Commander's Hall at the end of Ludwigstrasse

Situated to the west of the Commander's Hall, the **Theatinerkirche (32)** is a basilica in the style of the high Baroque and is considered by many to be one of the most beautiful churches in Munich. The building was a gift of Elector

Ferdinand Maria and his wife in gratitude for the birth of their long-awaited heir, Max Emanuel. After its consecration, the church (dedicated to St. Cajetan) was placed in the hands of the monks of the Theatine Order.

The overall conception of this domed, cruciform building is attributed to the Italian architect, Agostino Barelli, who supervised the first construction phase between 1663 and 1669. His successor, Enrico Zuccali, completed the 71-meter-high dome, erected the towers and decorated the interior. The facade was only completed in 1770 by Francois Cuvilliés in the late Rococo style. The marble figures in the facade niches (Saints Ferdinand, Adelheid, Maximilian and Cajetan) are the work of Roman Boos.

The magnificent facade of the Theatinerkirche

The interior, of which the high round arches of the barrel vaulting and the dome are the dominant features, is laid out according to Roman models: main nave with chapels, crossing cupola and semi-circular apse. The entire interior was painted white and lavishly ornamented with stucco work by Viscardi.

Crossing cupola of the Theatinerkirche

The high altar, an imposing columned structure, is crowned with figures of the four patron saints of the Electoral family. The altar painting is a work by Caspar de Crayer (1646), a pupil of Rubens. The black pulpit (1685–90) is by Andreas Faistenberger. Also worthy of note is the altar dedicated to St. Cajetan with a painting by J. von Sandrat (1667–71). The crypt under the high altar contains the massive stone sarcophagus of King Max II and his wife along with several bronze coffins containing members of the Wittelsbach family.

Located to the north of the Residence, the **Hofgarten (33)** was laid out according to the principles of Italian garden design during the reign of Maximilian I in 1613–17. The central point of this garden surrounded by arcades is the temple surmounted by the figure of the goddess Diana. On a warm summer's day, the café located in the west part of the garden is a pleasant place to watch enthusiasts playing petanque. To the east of the Hofgarten is the **Bavarian State Chancellery (Bayerische Staatskanzlei)**, which was designed by D. J. Siegert and completed in 1993. The centerpiece of this building complex, which provoked years of heated debate between the government and opposition, is the the restored dome of the former Museum of the Bavarian Army (1907).

In the north part of the Hofgarten is the **Prinz Carl Palais (34)**, which is used by the Bavarian government for ceremonial occasions. This palace, which now seems to be hemmed in by the heavy traffic of the Old City ring road, was built in the classical style by Karl von Fischer in 1804–06. Many of the works in the **State Museum of Egyptian Art (Staatliche Sammlung Ägyptischer Kunst) (35)** were acquired during the reigns of Albrecht V and Ludwig I. Located on the Hofgarten side of the Residence, this museum embraces every period of the history of ancient Egypt, and its outstanding exhibits include free-standing and relief sculpture, jewellery, sarcophagi, weapons and everyday utensils.

The State Museum of Egyptian Art is open Tues. from 9 a.m. to 9 p.m.; Weds. through Fri. from 9 a.m. to 4 p.m. and Weekends from 10 a.m. to 5 p.m.

"Temple of Diana" in the Hofgarten

Bronze nymph by Ludwig Schwanthaler on the west side of the Hofgarten

▼ *Prinz Carl Palais*

Centerpiece of the Bavarian State Chancellery: the dome of the former Museum of the Bavarian Army

The Residence – Ancestral Seat of the Wittelsbachs

For five centuries, the **Residence (36)** served as the ancestral seat of the dukes, prince-electors and, from 1806 to 1918, kings of Bavaria.

The history of the building goes back to 1385, at which time a citizens' revolt led the Wittelsbachs to give up their former seat, the "Alter Hof," and embark on the construction of a new fortified castle. This building, the "Neufeste," was almost completely demolished in the eighteenth century.

The present buildings of the Residence were erected between the sixteenth and nineteenth century, and are numbered among the finest achievements of the European Renaissance. The building complex contains six courtyards and can be regarded as falling into three main sections: the King's Building (Königsbau) facing Max-Joseph-Platz, the Old Residence (Alte Residenz) facing Residenzstrasse, and the Festival Hall Building (Festsaalbau) facing Hofgartenstrasse.

The Residence suffered severe damage during the war, but four decades of painstaking reconstruction have managed to restore most of its rooms to their former glory.

The building history of the Residence falls into six main phases:

1. The Reign of Albrecht V (1550–79).

The oldest building is the **Antiquarium** erected by Egckl in 1569–71. This is considered to be one of the largest and finest secular Renaissance buildings in Europe. The main hall is 69 meters in length and has a remarkable ornamented barrel vault. The walls are lined with classical busts and statues. The allegorical pictures lining the ceiling vault are the work of Peter Candid.

The Antiquarium in the Residence: one of Europe's finest and most beautiful secular buildings of the Renaissance

2. The Reign of Wilhelm V (1579–97).

Only a few sections of the construction work carried out in the reign of Wilhelm V have been preserved, namely the Elector's Chamber (Kurfürstenzimmer) in the upper storey of the Antiquarium, the east hall of the Grotto Court (Grottenhof) and the **Perseus Fountain (Perseusbrunnen)** in the middle of the Fountain Court (Brunnenhof). The last two of these are the work of Friedrich Sustris.

3. The Reign of Maximilian I (1597–1651).

At this time, the Residence attained its present layout, incorporating the "Neufeste" with the **Fountain Court (Brunnenhof)**, **Emperor's Court (Kaiserhof)** and **Apothecary Court (Apothekenhof)**. Buildings of this period comprise two chapels (Hofkapelle; Reiche Kapelle by Hans Krumpner, 1607), the **Wittelsbach Fountain** (Hubert Gerhard and Krumpner, 1611–14) in the Fountain Court (the loveliest of the courtyards), the octagonal fountain by the Antiquarium (1610), the four-winged building of the "Maximilian Residence" with the "Stone Rooms" around the Emperor's Court, the "Trier Room" with ceiling frescoes by Peter Candid, and the facade toward Residenzstrasse with Krumpner's "Patrona Bavariae," as well as the **Imperial Staircase (Kaisertreppe)** (1616) in the north wing, a late-Renaissance masterpiece.

Wittelsbach Fountain in the Fountain Court of the Residence

4. The Reigns of Karl Albrecht (1726–45) and Max III Joseph (1745–79).

In this period, the "Rich Rooms" ("Reichen Zimmer") around the Grotto Court received their remarkable Rococo décor, the work of Francois Cuvilliés. In 1751–53, he also provided the decoration of the **Cuvilliés-Theater** (Altes Residenztheater), which is considered to be the finest Rococo theater in the world.

5. The Reign of Ludwig I (1825–48).

Ludwig I was determined that Bavaria's new status as a kingdom (after 1806) should be reflected by splendid achievements in the fields of art, culture and architecture. This ruler had by far the most decisive influence on shaping the present-day appearance of the Residence. The construction of the **King's Building** (**Königsbau**; south side) and the **Festival Hall Building (Festsaalbau)** as a monumental north facade is closely linked with the name of Leopold von Klenze, whose role in the classical-style building phase was of decisive importance. Klenze used the Palazzo Pitti in Florence as a model when designing the facade of the King's Building (1826–35). In the **Nibelung Rooms (Nibelungensälen)**, there are superb frescoes depicting scenes of the German legend of the Nibelungs, these being the work of Schnorr von Carolsfeld and Hauschild.

Max-Joseph-Platz: King's Building of the Residence with the monument to Max Joseph I

The collections of the **Residence Treasury** (**Schatzkammer der Residenz**; begun under Albrecht V) include worked gold articles along with enamel, crystal and ivory work spanning the medieval and Rococo periods. Particularly outstanding exhibits include the Cross of Queen Gisela (ca. 1006), a statuette of St. George (ca. 1599) and the crown of the king of Bavaria (1806).

The "Battle Rooms" (Schlachtensäle) previously served as anterooms to the private chambers of Ludwig I. Unfortunately, nothing remains of the wall paintings depicting scenes of the legend of the Argonauts (by Schwanthaler and Schnorr von Carolsfeld), and these have been replaced by large battle paintings taken from the Hofgarten wing. Small side rooms contain exhibits of nineteenth-century European porcelain.

Having a length of about 250 meters, the Festival Hall Building (1832–42) with its massive two-tier portico of pilasters and columns was designed to satisfy the royal requirements for pomp and ceremony. The statues of the portico are the work of Ludwig Schwanthaler and depict the "Eight Spheres of Bavaria under the Wittelsbachs." The Throne Room of the Festival Hall Building – with the

The Residence Treasury: statuette of St. George (ca. 1599) ▶

form of a three-aisled basilica with Corinthian columns and galleries – is among the finest of Klenze's achievements. Sadly, it was almost entirely destroyed during the war.

6. The Twentieth Century.

On the site originally occupied by the Throne Room, the New Hercules Hall (Neue Herkulessaal) was built in the 1950s.

Among the comparable princely residences to be found in Germany, the Munich Residence is unchallenged in the way that it allows the present-day visitor to trace in detail the centuries of its architectural evolution, as well as the life styles and history of the dynasty that created it.

Opening hours of the Residence Museum and the Treasury:
Tues. through Sun. 10 a. m to 4:30 p. m.
Cuvilliés Theater:
Mon. through Sat. 2–5 p. m.; Sun. 10 a. m. to 5 p. m.

The **Royal Stables (Marstall) (37)** on Marstallplatz is an early work by Klenze dating from 1812–22. Formerly the court equestrian school, it now houses a theater (Theater im Marstall).

Just a few paces away in Maximilianstrasse, there is another theater, the **Kammerspiele (38)**, one of the loveliest Art Nouveau (Jugendstil) theaters in Germany, a work of M. Littmann and R. Riemerschmid dating from about 1900. Diagonally opposite is the Hotel Vier Jahreszeiten, a favorite resort of international celebrities.

The **National Theater (Nationaltheater) (39)** on Max-Joseph-Platz was built in the classical style by Karl von Fischer in 1811–18. Destroyed in the Second World War, it was rebuilt in its original form and reopened in 1963. To the north

The National Theater on Max-Joseph-Platz

of the National Theater stands the **Residence Theater (Residenztheater)**, which in 1948–51, was incorporated into the partially preserved outside walls of the Cuvilliés Theater; the latter theater was moved into the Apothecary Wing of the Residence.

The **Palais Törring (40)** – the former Main Post Office – located on Maximilianstrasse was built by I. A. Gunetzrhainer. However, in 1836–39, it was substantially altered by Klenze, who transformed it into an open columned hall with 12 Tuscan columns based on Florentine models. The frescoes are by J. G. Hiltensperger. In 1834, the building was acquired by the Post Office.

Maximilianstrasse, which leads away from Max-Joseph-Platz, is one of the city's three prestigious avenues dating from the nineteenth century. This street and **Theatinerstrasse** are the most elegant shopping areas in Munich.

From Theatinerstrasse to the Hofbräuhaus

Leaving Max-Joseph-Platz, we come back to Theatinerstrasse via Perusastrasse. Nearby is the **Kunsthalle der Hypo Kulturstiftung (41)**, an art gallery founded in 1985. Offering four or five excellent new exhibitions per year (ranging from Egyptian sculpture to works of the European avant garde), this gallery has rapidly established an important position for itself in the Munich cultural scene.

The Kunsthalle der Hypo Kulturstiftung is open daily from 10 a. m. to 6 p. m. (Thurs. until 9 p. m.).

Via Schrammerstrasse, we come to the **Münzhof (42)**. Of this large Renaissance complex of buildings (Wilhelm Egckl, 1563–67), only an arcaded courtyard with three-storied pergola has been preserved. Originally, the ground floor contained the stables of the Old Court, while the upper storey housed the library and art collection of Albrecht V.

The **Old Court (Alter Hof) (43)** served as the first residence of the Wittelsbachs from 1253 to 1474. Built by Ludwig the Severe after the division of Bavaria (1255), it reached the pinnacle of its fortunes under Ludwig the Bavarian, who was Holy Roman Emperor from 1328 to 1347. Since the seventeenth century, the Old Court has only been used as an administrative building and is now the headquarters of the city's tax office. Visitors are allowed into the attractive courtyard, but the building itself is not open to the general public. A clear impression of the original form of this building is provided by the model of the city in the Bavarian National Museum. A feature of the courtyard that is particularly worth seeing is the late-Gothic turret, nicknamed the "Monkey Tower" (Affenturm). A legend claims that, when Emperor Ludwig was a baby, he was seized by a monkey from the court menagerie, which carried him to the top of this tower and required considerable persuasion to bring him down again.

The **Hofbräuhaus (44)** located on the Platzl, a meeting place for tourists from all over the world, is virtually a compulsory part of any tour of Munich. After the Oktoberfest, it is the best-known institution of the city. It was founded in

The Old Court: the first residence of the Wittelsbachs

1589 by Wilhelm V to supply the needs of the court and its servants, and only in 1828 did the brewery become an inn. In spite of the flood of tourists, the Hofbräuhaus is still the "local" of many old Müncheners, who are happy to enjoy a jug or two with their friends, served in specially reserved beer mugs.

The Hofbräuhaus is the last stop on our tour of Munich's Old City. Via Orlandostrasse and Im Tal it's only a few minutes' walk back to our starting point, Marienplatz.

The Hofbräuhaus: one of Munich's most popular attractions

The unique atmosphere of a Munich beer garden

2 City Center (North West): From Königsplatz to the University

The massive square, **Königsplatz**, was conceived by Ludwig I as a cultural focal point of his "Athens on the Isar." Along with the buildings of Ludwigstrasse, it represents his most monumental contribution to Munich in its present form. Originally planned by Karl von Fischer in 1811, it was Leopold von Klenze who, a few years later, drew up the final design according to models from the classical world: the "Doric" Propyläen, the "Ionic" Glyptothek and the "Corinthian" State Museum of Classical Art.

During the Third Reich, the square was laid with stone slabs, so that it served as an appropriately "martial" setting for parades and ceremonies. These stones were removed in 1988.

Inspired by the Propylaea (Greek, "temple entrance") on the Athenian Acropolis, Klenze conceived the **Propyläen (45)**, which was built in 1846–62, as the entrance gateway to the new city of culture. The pediment sculptures on each side celebrate both the War of Independence fought by Greece against the Ottoman Empire, as well as Ludwig's son, Otto, who became King of Greece in 1832.

Klenze's first construction for Königsplatz was the **Glyptothek (46)**, which was erected between 1816 and 1830. It contains one of the most important sculpture collections to be found in Europe. Even while crown prince, Ludwig expressed his love of the culture of antiquity by employing agents to acquire Greek and

Königsplatz: the Propyläen and Glyptothek

Roman artworks. With the Glyptothek, Klenze created a worthy setting for these exceptional works. The building has a portico of Ionic columns and comprises four wings with a central open courtyard that serves to light the interior, as the exterior wall has no windows, being decorated instead with statues in niches.

Destroyed in the war (the sculpture collection was preserved), the Glyptothek was reopened in 1972.

Its finest works include:

Room II: the delightful "Barberini Faun" (ca. 220 B. C.), which is named after the place where it was found, the Palazzo Barberini in Rome.

Room IV: Mnesarete tomb relief (ca. 380 B. C.).

Rooms VII and IX: the west and east pediment sculptures from the Temple of Aegina (ca. 500 B. C.).
Room XIII: "The Youth with a Goose" (ca. 200 B. C.).

Opening hours of the Glyptothek:
Tues. & Weds. from 10 a. m. to 5 p. m.; Thurs. from 10 a. m.
to 8 p. m.; Fri.–Sun. from 10 a.m. to 2 p.m.
Nearest subway station: Königsplatz.

The "Barberini Faun" (ca. 220 B.C.) in the Glyptothek

The **State Museum of Classical Art (Staatliche Antikensammlung) (47)**, whose central section resembles a Greek temple of the Corinthian order, was completed in 1848 under the supervision of Georg Friedrich Ziebland. It now contains important collections of art and artefacts from the classical period.

At first, the building was used for art and industrial exhibitions. After suffering severe damage in the war, its reconstruction was completed in 1967.

On display are extensive collections of works in bronze, pottery, terracottas and smaller sculpture.

The main floor exhibition includes the famous Helikon-Lekythos (room I, display case D) and the Exekesias and Dionysus kraters (room II, display cases 11 and 12). In the lower storey (room X), the superbly wrought gold funeral wreath of Armento can be seen.

Opening hours of the State Museum of Classical Art:
Tues., Thurs.-Sun. 10 a. m. to 4:30 p. m.; Weds. 12 a. m. to
8:30 p. m. (free guided tour at 6 p. m. except on Public Holidays).
Nearest subway station: Königsplatz.

A krater by Exekesias.
Inset: Ship of Dionysus,
from ca. 530 B.C.
(Museum of Classical Art)

The **City Gallery in the Lenbach House (Städtische Galerie im Lenbachhaus) (48)** was built in 1887–91 by Gabriel von Seidl for the "painter prince," Franz von Lenbach, who made portraits of many famous figures, including Bismarck, Kaiser Wilhelm and Eleonora Duse.

Its style leans heavily on the models of the Florentine High Renaissance. The south wing contained the artist's studio, while the north wing was added in the 1920s. Since 1929, this villa has housed the extensive collections of the City Gallery, whose most important aspect is the documentation of painting in Munich from the late-Gothic period up to the twentieth century.

Ground floor: works from 1920 to the present (including Caspar-Filser, Klee, Schrimpf, Zimmermann), paintings of the Gothic and Baroque periods.

Upper floor: Munich "Romantics" and landscape painters of the first half of the nineteenth century; also works by Corinth, Spitzweg and Lenbach; Kandinsky collection; Blaue Reiter (Marc, Macke, Jawlensky, Münter).

Of particular interest are the acquistions of contemporary avant garde art: works by Beuys, Nitsch and Rainer are complemented by changing exhibitions.

In 1994, the area available for exhibitions was increased by the addition of the **Kunstbau Lenbachhaus** (changing exhibitions), whose entrance is to be found in the Königsplatz subway station.

Opening hours of the City Gallery in the Lenbach House:
Tues.-Sun. 10 a.m. to 6 p.m.;
Kunstbau, 10 a.m. to 6 p.m.
Nearest subway station: Königsplatz.

The Lenbach House, home of the City Gallery

"Show Your Wounds"
by Joseph Beuys

The famous Munich Agreement of 1938 was signed in the **State College of Music (Staatliche Hochschule für Music**; Arcisstrasse 12), Hitler's former Conference Building.

Karolinenplatz (49), which was built according to plans by Karl von Fischer in 1809–12, was largely modeled on the Place de l'Etoile in Paris. The obelisk in the center of the square was designed by Klenze and is a monument to the Bavarian soldiers who died during Napoleon's Russian campaign.

The two art galleries located to the north of Königsplatz (Barerstrasse no. 27 and 29) are among the most important galleries in Germany.

Karolinenplatz with its obelisk

The **Alte Pinakothek (50)** has a unique collection of works by Old German and Flemish masters. It also contains important works by the Dutch, French and Spanish schools. As a result, the Alte Pinakothek provides a comprehensive view of the most important currents in European painting between the fourteenth and eighteenth centuries. A large proportion of the works on show stem from the collections of the Wittelsbach rulers.

Ludwig I, a great lover of the arts, commissioned Leo von Klenze to design the Alte Pinakothek (built 1826–36), whose style is that of a Venetian Renaissance palace. The largest gallery built in the nineteenth century, it served as a model for museum buildings in Rome and Brussels. The statues of famous painters on the exterior as well as the frescoes of the interior were victims of bombing raids in the last war. The Alte Pinakothek was restored in the 1950s, so that its collections could be brought out of storage for exhibition.

Facade of the Alte Pinakothek

Here is a brief overview of the works on display:

Ground floor: Old German masters (Grien, Pacher), paintings of the sixteenth and seventeenth centuries (Jan and Peter Brueghel).

Upper floor: Old Dutch masters (van der Weyden, van Leyden), Old German masters (Dürer, Altdorfer), Italian painting (Giotto, Leonardo da Vinci, Raphael, Titian), Flemish painting (Rubens), Dutch painting (Rembrandt), French painting (Boucher, Chardin) and Spanish painting (El Greco, Velaszquez).

The informal style of the **Neue Pinakothek (51)** stands in striking contrast to the symmetrical palace architecture of the Alte Pinakothek opposite. It was built in 1975–81 by Alexander von Branca, and is Germany's largest post-war museum building (at a cost of DM 105 million). Grouped around two inner halls, the groundplan of the building has the form of figure "8" laid diagonally. All of the exhibition rooms are lit from above via so-called "dust roofs."

The site was previously occupied by a gallery built in the middle of the nineteenth century as a complement to the Alte Pinakothek. However, this building was so badly damaged in the war that it had to be demolished.

The art collection of the Neue Pinakothek comprises about 550 paintings and 50 sculptures from a period spanning the Rococo and Art Nouveau styles.

The exhibits include works dating from about 1800 (Goya), the early Romantic period (Caspar David Friedrich), French and German late Romanticism (Delacroix, Spitzweg), the "German Romans" (von Marées, Böcklin), the Impressionists (Manet, Cézanne, Gaugin, van Gogh, Corinth) and works of the Symbolist and Art Nouveau oeuvre (Klimt, Stuck, Toulouse-Lautrec).

Cafeteria and main entrance of the Neue Pinakothek

Information

The Neue Pinakothek is open
Tues. 10 a. m. to 8 p. m. (free guided tour at 6.30 p.m.
except on Public Holidays).
Weds. through Sun. 10 a.m. to 5 p.m.
Nearest subway station: Königsplatz / Streetcar 18.

East of Barerstrasse lies the **Student Quarter** with the Ludwig Maximilian University at its center. Its streets, such as Schelling-, Adalbert- and Türkenstrasse are characterized by a vast selection of bookshops, antique shops, cafés and pubs.

Munich's student population of over 100,000 is the largest in Germany. The **Ludwig Maximilian University (52)** (Geschwister-Scholl-Platz) alone has over 65,000 registered students. Founded at the behest of Ludwig I as the "Forum of Sciences," this building in the classical-Romantic style was erected in 1835–40 by Friedrich von Gärtner. In the first years of the present century, German Bestelmeyer added the Art Nouveau "T"-shaped extension (Amalienstrasse) with its central air well. This was the scene of the leaflet campaign of the opposition group, "White Rose," against the Nazi dictatorship. The leaflets displayed by the main entrance commemorate the leaders of this group, Hans and Sophie Scholl, who were executed in 1943.

Opposite the University (Professor-Hubert-Platz) are the Gregorianum Seminary – another of Gärtner's works dating from 1834–41 and the Max-Joseph-Stift, formerly an "Institute for the Education of Young Ladies." The unity of the two halves of the square is emphasized by the basin fountains, whose form echoes that of the fountains in St. Peter's Square.

Fountain in front of the University and the Ludwig Church

Handbills of the opposition group "White Rose" in the main entrance of the University

The monumentality of **Ludwigstrasse** was intended by Ludwig I to reflect the importance of the Kingdom of Bavaria. It is bounded by the Commander's Hall to the south and the Victory Gate to the north.

The basic concept stems from Leo von Klenze, who designed the classical buildings of the southern section (early Italian Renaissance style). His successor as court architect, Friedrich von Gärtner, was responsible for the buildings of the northern section (Roman-style forms).

The **Ludwig Church (Ludwigskirche) (53)**, with its combination of neo-Romanesque and classical elements was built in 1829–44 during the construction of the north part of Ludwigstrasse. Commissioned by Ludwig I, its planning and erection were the work of Friedrich von Gärtner.

The facade with its widely spaced towers is so oriented that it is not only angled toward Ludwigstrasse but also serves as an attractive ending to Schellingstrasse. The Ludwig Church seems to establish a counterpoint with the Theatinerkirche, owing to its site being diagonally opposite the latter's location at the north end of Ludwigstrasse. Indeed, Gärtner took the idea of a cruciform groundplan and two-tower front from the Theatinerkirche. The semi-circular niches on the facade contain figures by Ludwig Schwanthaler (Christ and the Evangelists, 1832–35). The round-arch motif of the portico is continued by the arcades on either side of the church, thus establishing a link between the church and neighboring secular buildings.

The interior is dominated by a monumental fresco of the Last Judgement (1836–40) by Peter Cornelius; after Michelangelo's painting of the same subject in the Sistine Chapel, it is one of the largest wall paintings in the world.

Located next to the Ludwigskirche, the **Bavarian State Library (Bayerische Staatsbibliothek) (54)** contains over five million volumes (the number increases daily) and is thus the largest general library of all German-speaking countries. Its collection includes valuable manuscripts as well as extensive specialist collections relating to Eastern Europe, the Orient and the Far East.

Entrance of the Bavarian State Library

This remarkably wide structure was built by Gärtner in 1834–39 on the commission of Ludwig I. Its style draws heavily on that of Italian palaces of the early Renaissance. The central section of the building is dominated by a massive stairway, on whose parapet are statues of great Greek thinkers: Thucydides, Homer, Aristotle and Hippocrates. Inside the building, the most impressive feature is the main staircase leading up to the brightly lit upper storey with its statues of Duke Albrecht V (founder of the court library) and Ludwig I.

The monumental **Victory Gate (Siegestor) (55)** was inspired by the Constantine Gate in Rome and was built by Gärtner in 1843–52. Ludwig I intended this to be a monument in honor of the Bavarian army. The gate is crowned by a bronze statue of Bavaria with a chariot pulled by four lions. The reliefs showing battle scenes also commemorate the Bavarian army. The relief-like medallions depict allegories of the regions of Bavaria.

The Victory Gate

After the Second World War, the gate was not fully restored, and a new inscription was added: "Consecrated to victory, destroyed by war, an admonition to peace."

The Victory Gate is the starting point of Leopoldstrasse, which is where the suburb of **Schwabing** begins. Once called the "Montmartre of Munich," it was a meeting place of authors like Thomas Mann, Frank Wedekind, Stefan George and Rilke, while the pub, "Simpl," was a favorite haunt of the poet Ringelnatz.

While it may no longer have the same cultural aura, the area still has its attractions, particularly Leopoldstrasse with its boutiques, street cafés and bars, which make it an ideal place for a summer stroll. However, suburbs such as Haidhausen and Westend now have a better claim to represent the Munich "scene."

City Center (North East): English Garden, Lehel, Bogenhausen

Prinzregentenstrasse, which was built at the turn of the present century during the reign of the Prince Regent, Luitpold, contains a number of impressive buildings: the Haus der Kunst, the Prinz Carl Palais, the Bavarian National Museum, the Schack Gallery and the Bavarian Ministry of Trade and Commerce (no. 28). This last major street project of the nineteenth century runs close by the English Garden, which starts just behind the **Haus der Kunst (56)** (Staatsgalerie Moderner Kunst; Prinzregentstrasse 1). The pseudo-classical building was erected as the "House of German Art" after Hitler's seizure of power. This monumental construction (160 meters long; 60 meters wide) with its colonnade of Doric columns was designed by P. L. Troost and completed in 1937.

The House of German Art achieved a certain notoriety by serving as the venue of the "Depraved Art" (Entartete Kunst) exhibition of 1937, aimed at ridiculing contemporary avant garde artists (e. g., Kokoschka, Dix, Klee, Beckmann).

Today, as the Staatsgalerie Moderne Kunst, it is one of the most renowned galleries of modern art, with over 450 excellent exhibits of twentieth-century art and regular exhibitions of modern European and non-European art.

Ground floor: Picasso, Munch, Kirchner, "Die Brücke," Cubism, Bauhaus and Constructivism, Klee, Surrealism (Ernst, Dali, Picasso), Beckmann, Macke, Kokoschka, Dix, Grosz, and abstract art of the 1940s, 1950s and 1960s.

Upper floor: Italian sculpture, new figurative painting, Abstract Expressionism and Pop Art, Photorealism, Baselitz, Christo and Beuys.

The Staatsgalerie Moderne Kunst is open Tues.-Sun. 10 a. m. to 5 p. m. (Thurs. until 8 p. m.) Nearest subway station: Odeonsplatz or Lehel.

The Haus der Kunst

The **English Garden (57)** is much more than the largest city park in Germany. Ask any Munich citizen what he or she finds especially attractive about the city and you can be sure that this garden will be high on the list. Starting from the Haus der Kunst, it is possible to walk or cycle through the new and old parts of the garden along the Isar as far as Freising without having to come in contact with the city traffic. Along with its well-known summer attraction – nude bathing along the Eisbach – the park offers a comprehensive cross-section of the Munich population; walkers, joggers, hippies, bankers enjoying their lunch-break, pensioners, tourists and embracing couples: in short, anyone and everyone.

On the suggestion of the later Count Rumford, the Prince Elector Karl Theodor had a "Military Garden" laid out along the Isar in 1789, which soon after, was opened to the public. A lake, the Kleinhesselohe See, was added shortly after this.

In 1789, J. Frey built the **Chinese Tower** as a vantage point for viewing the city and garden and as a covered bandstand. It burned down during the war and was

The Chinese Tower

reconstructed in 1951. The adjoining beer garden is a popular attraction in summer. Other recommended stopping points are the lake house on the Kleinhesseloher See and the Aumeister, a restaurant with a beer garden in the north part of the English Garden.

The **Monopteros**, a circular classical temple built by Klenze in 1837–38, offers a lovely view of the Old City.

The Monopteros

The contents of the **Bavarian National Museum (Bayerisches Nationalmuseum) (58)** partly stem from an exhibition of 1855 in the Herzog-Max-Burg, which soon proved too small to contain the rapidly growing collection.

The museum's function of displaying various epochs of history was imaginatively given visual form by its architect Gabriel von Seidl. While the interiors of the museum's individual sections were given the style of the same epoch as the objects to be displayed in them, their exteriors were given totally different, contrasting architectural styles. The diverse architectural types to be seen on the facade correspond to the historical sequence of the periods covered by the museum: Romanesque (east wing), early Baroque (tower with accentuated central building), Renaissance (west wing) and Rococo (west end).

In front of the east wing that was added in the 1940s, there is an equestrian monument to Prince Luitpold (A. Hildebrand). The west annex contains new collections (Neue Sammlung), while the north section has exhibitions devoted to prehistory (Prähistorische Staatsammlung).

The Bavarian National Museum is one of Germany's finest museums of European sculpture and arts and crafts. Its collections fall into two main sections:

The front of the Bavarian National Museum

The **Art History Collection (Kunstgeschichtliche Sammlung)** has displays of art and crafts from the early Middle Ages to the present century: Old German sculpture, tapestries, pottery, gold and silver work, miniatures, marquetry and stained glass (Kunsthistorisches Museum and Kunstgewerbemuseum).

The "Seon Madonna" (ca. 1430)

Alabaster statue of Judith (ca. 1512–14) by Conrad Meit

Crib (ca. 1750) from the North Tyrol

The **Folklore Collection (Volkskundliche Sammlung)** covers Bavarian ceramics, cribs, games, clocks and watches, and measuring instruments (Kulturhistorisches Museum). The best-known exhibits on the **ground floor** include works by Multscher (room 8), the Augsburg Weaving Room (room 9), the Passau Room (room 10), the Weissenburg Room (room 12), the Flanders Tapestry Room (room 13), the Riemenschneider Room (room 16), the Weapon Room (room 18), the Leinberger Room (room 21), the Landshut Room (room 39) and the closet from the Palais Tattenbach (room 41).

The **upper floor** has specialist collections of arts and crafts (porcelain, carved ivory, gold and silver work, marquetry, textiles, clocks and scientific instruments).

The exhibits in the **basement storey** provide interesting insights into country life in earlier times (rustic living rooms, furniture, crockery, clothes, glass, folk art). The museum's collection of cribs is particularly well-known (basement of the east wing).

**The Bavarian National Museum is open
Tues.-Sun. 9:30 a.m. to 5 p.m.
Nearest subway station: Lehel.**

The **Neue Sammlung** (State Museum of Applied Art) is housed in the study building of the west wing of the Bavarian National Museum. The collection of over 30,000 objects (crafts, industrial design, applied graphics) traces developments in the field of applied art. The exhibits comprise textiles, posters, pottery, furniture, porcelain and utensils of all kinds.

Throughout the year, the museum has changing exhibitions dealing with twentieth-century form and design.

**Opening times
of the Neue Sammlung:
Tues.-Sun. 10 a.m. to 5 p.m.
Nearest subway station: Lehel.**

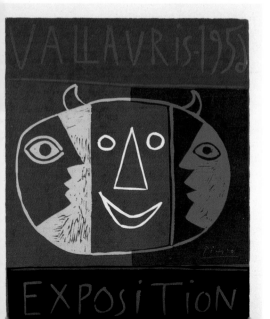

The "Vallauris" poster by Picasso (1956) is one of the treasures of the Neue Sammlung

A tour of the **Prehistoric Museum (Prähistorische Staatssammlung) (59)** presents a survey of Bavaria through the ages from the Old Stone Age to the early Middle Ages. Each epoch has a separate room devoted to it, with photo displays, slide projections, reconstructions, maps and models helping to make a visit to this museum both instructive and entertaining.

Thus, one gains insights into matters ranging from Roman life in Regensburg to the details of surgical techniques used by Celtic doctors (Obermenzinger Arztgrab).

**The Prehistoric Museum is open
Tue.-Sun. 9 a. m. to 4 p. m.
Nearest subway station: Lehel.**

Oriental face mask

The art collection of the **Schack Gallery (60)** (Prinzregentstrasse 9) provides an excellent survey of developments in nineteenth-century German painting (early Romanticism, Idealism, Post-Romanticism). Between 1858 and 1874, Count Adolf Friedrich von Schack acquired a remarkable collection of works by painters such as Böcklin, Lensbach, Feuerbach, Spitzweg and Marées that form the core of the exhibits of this interesting museum.

The architectonic and sculptural group comprising the **Angel of Peace (Friedens-engel) (61)** – the culminating point of Prinzregentenstrasse – dates from the turn of the century. The style of the Prince Regent Terrace is derived from Florentine garden design.

The lower section of Corinthian columns of the Friedensengel forms an open hall, and the corner columns have relief sculptures of famous figures. The monument was a donation of the city of Munich to commemorate the 25th anniversary of the Peace of Versailles. The golden Angel of Peace corresponds to the Nike (Winged Victory) of Olympia, who holds a palm branch in her right hand and a figure of armed Pallas Athena in her left.

The "Angel of Peace" adorning Prinzregentenstrasse

The "painter prince," Franz von Stuck, designed for his own use the **Villa Stuck (62)** (Prinzregentenstrasse 60), which combines classical and Art Nouveau elements. It was constructed in 1897/98 and, a few years later, a studio building similar in style was added.

The decoration and furnishings of the interior are quite unique, with Stuck's living quarters on the ground floor being especially remarkable. The Villa Stuck has changing exhibitions relating to Art Nouveau, classical modernism, applied art and contemporary art.

The Museum Villa Stuck is open Tues.-Sun. 10 a. m. to 5 p. m. (Thurs. until 8 p. m.). Nearest subway station: Prinzregentenplatz.

The Villa Stuck: one of Munich's finest Art Nouveau (Jugendstil) buildings

It's worth taking a stroll through the elegant streets close to the Villa Stuck (e. g., Möhlestrasse and Maria-Theresia-Strasse), an exclusive district that only embassies, businesses and celebrities can comfortably afford.

4 Haidhausen – Museum Island, Gasteig Arts Center, Maximilianeum

The **German Museum (Deutsches Museum) (63)** located close to the Isartor streetcar station is one of the most important and popular (1.5 million visitors per year) museums of science and technology in the world. About 17.000 objects demonstrating the principles and development of science and technology are to be found over an exhibition area of over 45.000 square-meters.

Founded at the beginning of the nineteenth century by the engineer, Oskar von Miller, the collections were moved the present building complex (designed by Gabriel von Seidl) on an island of the Isar in 1925.

The German Museum is anything but a "dry" assembly of exhibits; indeed, one of the reasons for its popularity is its "hands on" approach, which allows the visitor literally to "get to grips" with the objects on display. Important scientific principles and processes are demonstrated by means of experimental devices, films, diagrams, dioramas and working models. The museum's library contains over 700.000 books and journals, as well as a large collection of plans, documents, patents and catalogues.

The aviation and spaceflight section of the German Museum

The sheer size and range of the German Museum rules out the possibility of seeing everything in one visit, so that it is best to select in advance a few sections of particular interest. The following list covers the most popular departments:

The lifelike recreation of a coal mine (basement), navigation (including the first German submarine), rail travel, motor vehicles, aviation and space travel (from Lilienthal to vertical take-off), and astronomy.

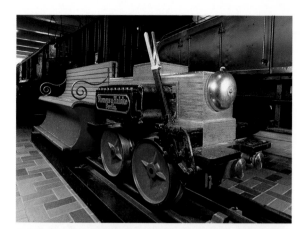

*The first
electric
locomotive
(1879)*

Demonstration of "Faraday's cage"

The most modern planetarium in the world in the adjoining **Forum der Technik** is also well worth a visit. Another recently added attraction is the **IMAX** cinema in the former Kongresshalle.

**The German Museum is open
daily from 9 a.m. to 5 p.m.
Nearest subway station: Isartor.**

Munich's Hellabrunn Zoo

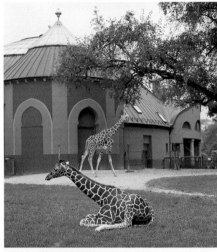

Located opposite the German Museum, the **Müllersches Volksbad (64)** (Rosenheimer Strasse 1) is an indoor swimming pool (with steam bath) in the Art Nouveau (Jugendstil) style built in 1897–1901 and designed by K. Hocheder.

Just a few paces away is the **Gasteig Arts Center (Kulturzentrum am Gasteig) (65)**, a modern complex completed in 1985, which now houses the municipal library, the Richard Strauss Conservatory, an adult education center and the Philharmonie concert hall.

Seating an audience of up to 2500, this last is the largest and most architecturally impressive hall of the arts complex. The "Black Box," "Kleine Konzertsaal" and "Carl-Orff-Saal" are used for concerts, plays and lectures.

The Gasteig Arts Center

Situated about 500 meters to the north of the Gasteig complex, the **Maximilianeum (66)**, seat of the Bavarian State Parliament (Landtag) and Senate, marks the end of Maximilianstrasse. Commissioned by King Maximilian, it was built in 1857–74 by Friedrich Bürklein as the "Institute for the Education and Instruction of Gifted Students."

The wide central section with Renaissance-style round arches is flanked on both sides by two-storied wings that take the form of loggias with three-storied corner towers. The original paintings in the "Attika" were replaced by mosaics on a gold ground in 1902.

The Maximilianeum – Seat of the Bavarian State Parliament

Olympic Center and BMW Museum

The **Olympia Park (67)** – now a favorite place for leisure and relaxation – was created for the 20th Summer Olympic Games held in Munich in 1972. This large park (area, almost 3 square-kilometers) was laid out on the former Oberwiesenfeld, which was once used as a parade ground and, later, as a military airport.

The best-known symbol of the Olympia Park is the 290-meter-high **Olympia Tower**. On a clear day, the Alps can be seen from its viewing platform, while its revolving restaurant provides a complete bird's-eye view of the city every hour or so.

The Olympic Stadium, the Olympic Hall, the Olympic Swimming Pool and the remarkable net-like roof construction made of acrylic glass were designed by the architect's company, Behnisch and Partner.

The oval **Olympic Stadium** with room for 78.000 spectators is now used for football matches (F. C. Bayern Munich), athletics meetings and pop concerts. The Olympia Hall was conceived as a multi-purpose hall seating up to 14.000 people and is now the venue of events such as the Munich Six-Day Race as well as concerts of various kinds.

The south part of the sporting complex contains a lake (Olympiasee), next to which is the **Theatron**, an open-air stage that is the venue of numerous events, particularly in the summer ("Rock Summer," "Singats").

The 52-meter-high hill, the Olympiaberg, is made of rubble gathered during the great reconstruction effort (called the "Rama Dama," slang for "we'll clear up") after the Second World War.

To the north of the Middle Ring Road (Mittlere Ring) stands the **Olympic Village**, the scene of the terrorist kidnapping of the Israeli Olympic team (a monument has been erected in Conollystrasse). Many of the apartments are now used as student halls of residence.

In summer, the Olympic Park plays host to the alternative "Tollwood Festival," an event that includes many concerts and a large market.

The Elevator, Viewing Platform and Revolving Restaurant of the Olympia Tower are open daily from 9 a.m to 12 p.m. (admission till 11.30 p.m.) Nearest subway station: Olympiazentrum.

View of the buildings in the Olympia Park

The **BMW-Hochhaus**, the high-rise headquarters of BMW, is a distinctive feature of the Munich skyline. Completed in 1973, this unusual architectural construction designed by Karl Schwanzer has the form of four cylinders grouped around an open shaft.

In striking contrast to the headquarters building, the **BMW Museum (68)** ("Time Horizon"; Petuelring 130) is housed in a windowless, silver-colored concrete dome. The museum, whose layout is completely redesigned every 5 years or so, traces the major developments in the history of BMW stretching back almost 80 years: the company's airplane engines, motorcycles and automobiles are presented against a background of the periods in which they were con-

*BMW Headquarters
and BMW Museum*

*BMW 303 and
AM4 limousines
(ca. 1930)*

BMW 502

structed. Excellent visual displays help to bring to life spectacular events of the past and present, while other exhibits cast light on technological developments of the future.

The BMW Museum is open
daily from 9 a. m. to 5 p. m.
Nearest subway station: Petuelring or Olympiazentrum.

6 Nymphenburg Castle

The former summer residence of the rulers of Bavaria is located in the west part of the city in the middle of one of Munich's most beautiful parks. Five generations of Wittelsbach rulers were involved in the construction of this Baroque castle.

The building of **Nymphenburg Castle (69)** began in the reign of the Elector Ferdinand Maria: overjoyed by the birth of his son and heir, Max Emanuel, he had the central section built for his wife in the style of an Italian villa (Agostino Barelli, 1664–74). In about 1700, Max Emanuel commissioned Enrico Zuccali and Antonio Viscardi to extend the castle by adding galleries and pavilions. The central section owes its present appearance to the efforts of Josef Effner, who

Nymphenburg Castle (east facade)

in 1715, designed the pilasters, arched windows and busts that now grace the exterior. A few years later, the south section of the castle was added to serve as the court stables. As a counterpart, the orangerie was added to the north.

Below are listed the most important rooms of the castle:

Central section: Stone Hall (Steinerner Saal; 1755–57) with ceiling frescoes by J. B. and F. Zimmermann (Homage to the Goddess Flora); the Rococo stucco work is based on designs by Cuvilliés.

North wing: Wood paneling by J. A. Pichler in the first anteroom, Brussels tapestries (ca. 1700) in the Gobelinzimmer, Max Emanuel's "Gallery of Beauties" (Schönheitsgalerie), Heraldry Room and former bedroom with paintings by J. Werner.

South wing: Anteroom and bedroom with ceiling paintings by A. D. Triva, "Chinese Varnished Chamber" (redesigned by Cuvilliés the Elder in 1763–64), the gallery of paintings of Bavarian castles (ca. 1750), and the famous "Gallery of Beauties" of Ludwig I with portraits of 36 beautiful women from all levels of Munich society. These include the dancer, Lola Montez, whose attractions proved irresistible to the king and were to contribute to his eventual downfall.

The **Castle Garden** was greatly enlarged in the eighteenth century and was laid out in the French style (using Versailles as a model) by Girard from 1715 onward. As the more natural style of the English park became fashionable in the nineteenth century, Sckell remodeled the garden according to the tenets of English landscaping while retaining the main elements of the Baroque garden.

The **Amalienburg**, a hunting lodge built by Francois Cuvilliés in about 1740, is considered to be a perfect example of court Rococo architecture. The circular Hall of Mirrors (with silver ornament on a blue background) with its symbolic hunting scenes is quite unique. Along with the Rest Room and Hunting Room with their silver and gold decoration, the kitchen decorated with Dutch tiles is a truly exquisite creation.

The Amalienburg – Rococo architecture at its finest

The **Badenburg** is one of the first heated indoor baths to be built in modern times. Built in 1719–21 by Josef Effner, the two-storied building provided bathing facilities for the court society of Max Joseph. The main hall is ornamented with stucco fruits and mussel shells, and the ceiling painting "Apollo in the Sun Chariot" is the work of J. Amigoni.

Effner also designed the **Pagodenburg**, a pavilion with a cruciform groundplan, which served as a place of repose for members of court society. The chinoiserie of the rooms reflects the fashion for oriental decoration prevailing at the time, while the exterior is ornamented with masks of Bacchus, Flora, Neptune and Ceres.

The **Hermitage of Mary Magdalen (Magdalenenklause)** was built in 1725–28 by Effner as a retreat for the ageing Elector Max Emanuel. Deliberately given the form of a partial ruin, this "place of penitence" has elements of Romanesque, Gothic and also Moorish architecture. The ceiling painting in the chapel showing scenes from the life of Mary Magdalen is the work of N. G. Stubner.

The Baroque waterfall, the "Grosse Kaskade," by the west entrance to the garden was designed by Effner; the marble covering is by Cuvilliés.

The **Marstall Museum** in the south wing of the castle, i. e., the former court stables, has an interesting collection of ceremonial carriages, sleighs, harnesses and saddlery that recalls the heyday of the Wittelsbachs. The most famous exhibit is the splendid carriage of Ludwig II.

The **Porcelain Museum** is also located in the south wing. The pieces on show comprise a comprehensive history of the products of the Nymphenburg porcelain manufactory (founded in 1761), which is based in the north-east section of the round tower in front of the castle.

The **Museum of Mankind and Nature** in the north wing of the castle offers several different exhibitions throughout the year.

Opening hours:

Castle, Gallery of Beauties and Amalienburg:
Tues.-Sun. 10 a. m. to 12:30 p. m. and 1:30 to 4 p. m.
(October through March);
Tues.-Sun. 9 a. m. to 12:30 p. m. and 1:30 to 5 p. m.
(April through September).

Badenburg, Pagodenburg and Magdalenenklause:
Tues.-Sun. 10 a. m. to 12:30 p. m. and 1:30 to 5 p. m.
(April through September).

Marstall Museum and Porcelain Museum:
Tues.-Sun. 10–12 a. m. and 1–4 p. m.
(October through March);
Tues.-Sun. 9–12 a. m. and 1–5 p. m.
(April through September).

Museum of Mankind and Nature:
Tues.-Sun. 9 a. m. to 5 p. m.

Streetcar no. 12 or
bus no. 41.

The **Botanical Garden (70)** in the north part of the Nymphenburg Park (Menzingerstrasse 65) is one of the most beautiful gardens in Germany, offering an astonishing variety of plants. It contains a large arboretum of deciduous and evergreen trees, an alpine garden, a fern garden and a rhododendron grove, as well as sections devoted to herbs and medicinal plants, genetics and ecology. The greenhouses contain exotic specimens, such as orchids, cacti and carnivorous plants.

Opening hours of the Botanical Garden:
Nov.-Jan. 9 a. m. to 4:30 p. m.
Feb., March, Oct. 9 a. m. to 6 p. m.
April, Sept. 9 a. m. to 6 p. m.
May-Aug. 9 a. m. to 7 p. m.
Streetcar no. 12.

Oktoberfest and Theresienwiese

The Oktoberfest, the biggest public (and beer) festival in the world, begins at 12 a. m. on the penultimate Saturday of September when the Lord Mayor of Munich taps open the first barrel with the words "Ozapft is" ("It's open") and the event's "landlords" (Wiesnwirte) enter in procession.

The liquid and solid delights of the festival attract millions of tourists from all over the world to the **Theresienwiese (71)** where it is held.

The history of the Oktoberfest goes back to the celebrations on the occasion of the wedding of the later King Ludwig I and the Princess of Sachsen-Hildburghausen in 1810.

At the time of its erection, the enormous statue of **Bavaria** that seems to preside over the event was the largest monumental statue in the world. Based on designs by Ludwig Schwanthaler, it was cast in bronze by Oskar von Miller in 1844–50. A climb up the interior stairway is rewarded by a lovely view of the city.

The figure of Bavaria rises high above the Ruhmeshalle (Hall of Fame), a three-winged Doric marble columned hall built by Klenze in about 1850. Its interior, which contains busts of 77 prominent Bavarians, is the work of Ludwig Schwanthaler.

Nearest streetcar stop:
Hackerbrücke
Nearest subway station:
Theresienwiese.

Munich's **Trade Fair Center (Messegelände)** is currently located close to the Theresienwiese, but there are plans to move it to a new site on the former airport of München-Riem.

Munich's Oktoberfest

The palace and gardens of Schleissheim date from the 17th and 18th centuries, and are located on the eastern edge of the Dachauer Moss.

The **Old Palace**, to the west of the New Palace, is a relatively modest Renaissance country mansion with two corner towers and an outdoor staircase, built for the Prince Elector Maximilian between 1617 and 1623. Behind it are the storerooms and stables of the farm that once belonged to his father, Duke Wilhelm.

After having been severely damaged during the war, the Old Palace was rebuilt and now houses a branch of the Bavarian National Museum.

The **New Schleissheim Palace** consists of a central wing, arcades, and side-pavilions, and was built between 1701 and 1704 by Henrico Zuccalli, originally as only the first part of a palace with four wings. The lord of the palace, Prince Elector Max II Emanuel, having recently defeated the Turks was at the zenith of his power, the dazzling expression of which was to have been his own "Versailles". However, political and pecuniary problems caused this ambitious project to be postponed, and work was only resumed in 1719 under Joseph Effner; it was mainly completed in 1726. The façade was redesigned by Klenze, for Ludwig I, and following its destruction in the second world war was rebuilt in the way Effner originally had in mind.

The interior of the palace is a masterpiece. Its attraction lies in its mixture of the late baroque and the first beginnings of rococo. The scenes illustrated in the frescoes and stucco work mainly relate to the wars against the Turks.

The interior decoration of the magnificent rooms, the artistic execution of which is in no way inferior to Nypmphenburg, was designed by Effner, who had a team of famous Bavarian artists at his disposal: Cuviliés the Elder (designs), Zimmermann (stucco work), Asam, Beich, and Amigone (painting), and Stuber (ornamentation) all worked on this project.

In the Baroque Gallery, now a branch of the Bavarian State Collections of Paintings, Max Emanuel had already hung some of the most important paintings from the Wittelsbach collections. The pictures now on display are mainly those for which there is no room in the Alte Pinkothek. The collection includes works from the Flemish and Dutch Schools (Rubens, van Dyck and van Goyen), the Italian baroque period (Carracci and Furini), and by baroque painters from France, Spain, and Germany.

The baroque **Palace Park**, with its cascade, was laid out from 1720 onwards to plans by D. Girard, with the Lustheim mansion forming the distant "point de vue".

Lustheim mansion had already been built between 1684 and 1688 by Zuccalli to celebrate the marriage of Prince Elector Max Emanuel to Maria Antonia, the Emperor's daughter. The ground floor consists of a main hall, rising into the second floor, adjoined by ten "cabinets" at the sides. The frescoes celebrate Diana, the goddess of the hunt.

This mansion contains the **Ernst Schneider Collection of Meissen Porcelain**.

The ground floor comprises a two-storied main hall with ten smaller rooms adjoining it. The frescoes celebrate Diana, goddess of hunting.
The castle contains a superb **Meissner Porcelain Museum (Meissner Porzellansammlung Ernst Schneider im Schloss Schleissheim)**.

"New" Schleissheim Castle (east facade)

Opening hours:

Altes Schloss:
Tues.-Sun. 10 a.m. to 5 p.m.
Neues Schloss, Schloss Lustheim, Meissner Porcelain Museum:
Tues.-Sun. 10 a.m. to 12:30 p.m. and 1:30 to 5 p.m.
(April through September);
10 a.m. to 12:30 p.m. and 1:30 to 4 p.m.
(October through March)

Nearest streetcar stop: Oberschleissheim.

Tips and Adresses from A to Z

Emergency Services
Police Tel. 110
Fire Brigade Tel. 112
Ambulance Tel. 19222
Doctor on Emergency Call
Tel. 558661
Pharmacy (all-night service)
Tel. 594475

Tourist Information
Fremdenverkehrsamt München
Postfach
80313 München
Tel. (089) 2330300
(information, brochures, accomodation
service).
Branches in:
– Main Railway Station (Hauptbahnhof)
Tel. 2330300 (no room reservations by
telephone)
Airport (Flughafen) Tel. 97592815
(no room reservations by telephone)
– City Center (Rindermarkt 5)

Accomodation/Room Reservations
Via the Fremdenverkehrsamt (see above
under "Tourist Information")

ADAC (Automobile Breakdown Service)
Ridlerstrasse 35, Tel. 51950

Airport
Information Tel. 97521313

Annual Events
January, February: Fasching (Carnival)
– particularly Faschingssonntag (the
Sunday before Ash Wednesday) until
Faschingsdienstag (Shrove Tuesday),
with Dance of the Market Women at the
Viktualienmarkt.
March: Start of the "Strong Beer"
(Starkbier) season (Nockherberg-
Ausschank).
April: Spring Festival (Frühlingsfest) on
the Theresienwiese; Auer Dult market
(end of April) on Mariahilfplatz.
May: Auer Dult market (until early
May). Procession through the city cele-
brating the Feast of Corpus Christi
(Fronleichnam) on the second Sunday
after Pentecost. Beer festival (Maibock-
ausschank) of the Munich breweries.
June: Start of the Nymphenburg Sum-
mer Concert series.
July: Film Festival; Opera Festival;
Concerts in the Fountain Court of the
Residence; Auer Dult market (until
early August).
August: Series of events in the Olympia
Park (Theatron).

September: Oktoberfest (from the third
Saturday of the month).
October: Auer Dult market and fair
(Mariahilfplatz)
December: Christmas markets (see
under "Markets")

Auer Dult
A traditional market held three times
per year (May, July, October) on the
square in front of the Mariahilfkirche.
Well worth a visit as the many stands
and stalls offer a great variety of goods,
ranging from typical "flea-market"
wares to antiques, porcelain and a wide
variety of household articles. The market also has a fair with different rides,
while sausages and roasted almonds are
among the "eatables" on offer.

Bavaria Film Studios
Guided tours give visitors a chance to
take a look behind the scenes of Germany's famous movie and TV studios.
Stunts, special effects, figures from the
film "The Never-Ending Story" and a
visit to a submarine (used in the film,
"The Boat") are all part of the fun
(advance booking necessary).
Bavariafilmplatz 7
Tel 64992304

Beer Gardens
Just a small selection: the "Hirschgarten" close to the streetcar stop, Laim, is
especially pretty, as are the "Chinesi-
scher Turm" (in the English Garden),
the "Aumeister" (in the north section of
the English Garden), the "Flaucher"
(on the Isar, close to the subway station,
Brudermühlestrasse) and the
"Augustiner" (Arnulfstrasse 52, close to
the Main Railway Station).

Botanical Garden
Menzinger Strasse 65 (see Text)

Bicycle Hire
Aktiv-Rad, Hans-Sachs-Strasse 7,
Tel. 266506
Radl Gipp, Kirchenstrasse 23,
Tel. 479846

Camping
"Langwieder See,"
Eschenrieder Str. 119,
Tel. 8641566
"Thalkirchen," Zentralländstrasse 49,
Tel. 7231707
"Obermenzing," Lochhauser Str. 59,
Tel. 8112235
(In all cases, March to October).

Carpooling/Lifts
Känguruh, Amalienstrasse 87,
Tel. 19444
ADM, Lämmerstrasse 4, Tel. 19440

Church Services
Times of services can be found in the
monthly booklet, "München im..."
or in the Friday editions of local
newspapers.

Concerts
For lovers of classical music, Munich has
a great deal to offer (if you are lucky
enough to get tickets!). Details of forth-
coming concerts and ticket offices are
listed in local newpapers and in
"München im..." (see under General
Information).
For rock, pop and jazz concerts, the free
fortnightly calendar of events, "in münchen," is recommended.

Consulates
Austria,
Ismaninger Strasse 136, Tel. 9210900
France,
Möhlstrasse 5, Tel. 4194110
Great Britain,
Bürkleinstrasse 10, Tel. 211090
Italy,
Möhlstrasse 3, Tel. 4180030
The Netherlands,
Nymphenburger Strasse 1, Tel. 5459670
Spain,
Oberföhringer Strasse 45, Tel. 293004
Switzerland,
Brienner Strasse 14, Tel. 2866200
United States,
Königinstrasse 5, Tel. 28880

Cultural Institutes
Institut Francais,
Kaulbachstrasse 13, Tel. 2866280
Amerika-Haus,
Karolinenplatz 3, Tel. 5525370
Goethe-Institut,
Helene-Weber-Allee 1, Tel. 159210
British Council,
Rumfordstrasse 7, Tel. 2900860
Italienisches Kulturinstitut,
Hermann-Schmid-Strasse 8,
Tel. 7463210
Spanisches Kulturinstitut,
Marstallplatz 7, Tel. 2907180

General Information
The monthly booklet, "München im..."
contains details of all important events,
opening hours, hotels, etc.
The fortnightly free booklet,
"in münchen," provides a calendar for
cinemas, theaters and concerts. It can
be picked up at cinemas, restaurants,
hotels, etc.

Guided Tours
(Selection)
– Münchner Stadtrundfahrten OHG,
Tel. 1204248
Short tours daily at 10 a. m.
and 2:30 p. m.
Longer tours Tues.-Sun. at 10 a. m.
Depart from Bahnhofsplatz
(in front of the Hertie department store)
– City Hopper Touren:
city tours by bicycle, Tel. 2721131
– Radius Touristik im Hauptbahnhof:
Munich by tram, by bicycle and on foot,
Tel. 596113
– Spurwechsel: city tours by bicycle,
Tel. 6924699
– Stadtreisen in München e. V.:
Munich on foot, by tram, by bicycle,
Tel. 2718940

Libraries
– Bayerische Staatsbibliothek
Ludwigstr. 16, Tel. 286380
– Staatbibliothek Am Gasteig
Rosenheimer Strasse 5, Tel. 48098313
(Opening times in "München im...")

Lost Property Offices
City Lost Property Office
(Städtisches Fundbüro),
Ruppertstrasse 19, Tel. 23300
Main Railway Station (Hauptbahnhof),
Tel. 13080
Post Office (Bundespost),
Arnulfstrasse 195, Tel. 55990
Streetcar (S-Bahn Ostbahnhof,
counter no. 8),
Tel. 557575

Markets
– Viktualienmarkt (see Text)
– Christmas Markets: "Christkindl-
markt" on Marienplatz (December);
other Christmas markets can be found
in Schwabing (Münchner Freiheit) and
Haidhausen (Weissenburger Platz).
– Auer Dult (see above).

Museums
Museums not described in the text
include the following:
– Staatliche Graphische Sammlung
(drawings and prints from the fifteenth
to the twentieth century)
Meiserstrasse 10, Tel. 28927650
(subway station Königsplatz)
Tues., Weds. 10 a. m. to 1 p. m.,
2 to 4:30 p. m.
Thurs. 10 a. m. to 1 p. m., 2–6 p. m.;
Fri. 10 a. m. to 12:30 p. m.
– Museum für Abgüsse Klassischer Bild-
werke (plaster casts of classical statuary)
Meiserstrasse 10, Tel. 28927691
(subway station Königsplatz)
Mon.-Fri. 10 a. m. to 5 p. m.

– Museum für Völkerkunde (Ethnological Museum, with a large collection of arts and crafts from all over the world) Maximilianstrasse 42, Tel. 2101360 (subway station Lehel)
– Paläontologisches Museum (Museum of Palaeontology, with prehistoric fossils and remains). Richard-Wagner-Strasse 10, Tel. 5203361 (subway station Königsplatz) Mon.-Thurs. 8 a.m. to 4 p.m., Fri. 8 a.m. to 2 p.m.
– Staatliche Münzsammlung (City Coin Museum) Residenzstrasse 1, Tel. 227221 (subway station Odeonsplatz) Tues.-Sun. 10 a.m. to 4:30 p.m.
– Deutsches Theatermuseum (German Theater Museum) Galeriestrasse 4a and 6, Tel. 2106910 (subway station Odeonsplatz) Tues.-Sun. 10 a.m. to 4 p.m.
– Jüdisches Museum München (Museum of Jewish Culture) Maximilianstrasse 36, Tel. 297453

Parks
Along with the English Garden, there are several attractive parks in the city, e.g., the Hirschgarten (with beer garden), the Olympia Park and the Nymphenburger Schlosspark.

Post
The Post Office (Postamt) in the Telegraph Office (Telegrafenamt) opposite the east side of the Main Railway Station (Hauptbahnhof) has extended opening hours:
Mon.-Fri. 6 a.m. to 10 p.m.; weekends and public holidays, 7 a.m. to 10 p.m.

Railway Information
Train information, Tel. 19419

Swimming
Particularly outstanding among the city's numerous bathing facilities are the "Müllersches Volksbad" (Art Nouveau baths), the indoor Olympic Swimming Pool (Olympiaschwimmhalle) and, particularly for children, the "Cosimabad" (indoor pool with wave pool).
The opening hours can be found in the monthly booklet, "München in." (see under the heading, "General Information").
Several large and small lakes are within easy striking distance from Munich, e.g., Ammersee, Lake Starnberg, Wesslinger See and Langwieder See.

Taxi
Central switchboard, Tel. 21610 or 19410

Telephone
Area code for Munich: 089

Theaters
Munich has a wide range of excellent theaters. Program details can be found in the local press and the information booklets, "in münchen" and "München im…" (with ticket offices).

Trade Fairs
Munich is Germany's most important center for trade fairs, including the CBR, ISPO, IHM, "Fashion Week" (Modewoche) and "Home and Handwork" (Heim und Handwerk). For details, see "München im…"

Transport
Munich has a good local transport system of subway trains (U-Bahn) and streetcars (S-Bahn) operated by the MVV. The most economical way to travel in the city is to buy a day-ticket (Tageskarte). Family tickets (Familienkarte) are also available. These are valid for the inner city transport network. Those on a longer visit who travel less frequently on public transport might choose a Streifenkarte, which is valid for several trips over an extended period of time.
Leisure areas close to Munich, such as the Ammersee or Lake Starnberg, can be easily reached by streetcar.
MVV central information, Tel. 210330

Youth Hostels
DJH-Gästehaus, Miesingstrasse 4, Tel. 7236550
DJH München, Wendl-Dietrich-Strasse 20, Tel. 131156
DJH Pullach (Near Munich), Burg Schwaneck, Tel. 7930643
CVJM, Landwehrstrasse 13, Tel. 5521410
Haus International, Elisabethstrasse 87, Tel. 120060

Zoo
The Tierpark Hellabrunn is said to be the first "Geo-Zoo" of the world, with the animals being grouped according to the region from which they originate. Owing to the spacious enclosures, the animals live in an environment closely resembling their natural habitat. Hellabrunn is particularly renowned for its success in breeding animals belonging to threatened sppecies.
Tierparkstrasse 30, Tel. 625080 (subway station Thalkirchen) April-Sept. 8 a.m. to 6 p.m.; Oct.-March 9 a.m. to 5 p.m.

Index

The numbers in paratheses refer to the numbers on the city map.

Schnellbahnen im Münchner Verkehrs- und Tarifverbund

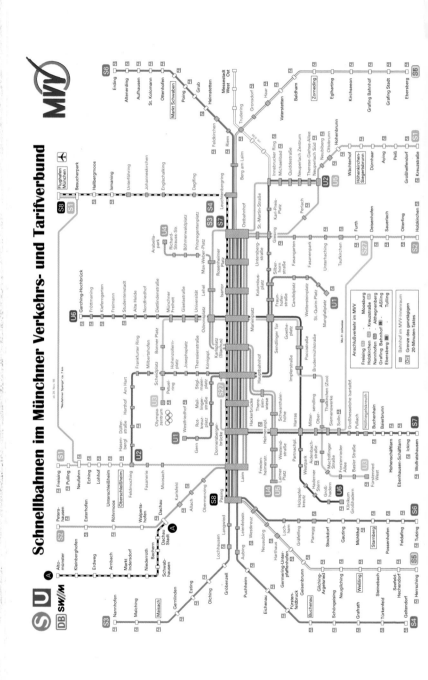

MÜNCHEN
INNERER BEREICH

350 m

- ✝ Kirche
- ☖ Denkmal
- Ⓤ U-Bahn
- Ⓢ S-Bahn
- ⓘ7 Sehenswürdigkeit

Ⓢ Moosach

MOOSACH

Georg-Brauchle-

Amphion-park

Wintrichring

Dachauer Str.

Landshuter Allee

Oly
h

Ⓤ

Westfriedhof (in Bau)

Olympia-Stadion 67 Coube
platz

Werner-von-Linde-Halle

OLYMPIAPARK

St. Mauritius

Westfriedhof

Garten-anlage

Gartenanlage

Baldur-

str.

Borstei

Olympia Radstadion

Nederlinger Str.

Baldur-

Dante-

Rosa-Luxemburg-Platz

Menzinger

Nederlinger Str.

Nederlinger Str.

Wertach-platz

Sigenot-platz

Dantepark

Mittlerer Ring

NEDERLING

Nymphenburger Kanal

Klug

Gern (in Bau)

70 Botanischer Garten

V. Goebel-Platz

L-Ferdinand-Platz

GERN

St.-Galler-Str.

Dom-Pedro-

Dom- Pedro-Str.

Leonrod-Platz

Schwe

Porz. Manuf.

Tizian-platz

Nördliche Auffahrts-

altee

altee

Volkart

Leonrod-

str.

Schloß Nymphenburg

Hubertus-

Südliche Auffahrts-

Waisenhausstr.

69 NYMPHENBURG

Notburga

Schloß park

Roman-

Rondell Neuwittelsbach

Ruffin str.

Amalienburg

str.

Roman-platz

Nibelungenstr.

Washingtonstr.

Volkan

Platz der Freiheit

Ⓤ

Arnulf-

Wotanstr.

Hirschbergstr.

Steuben-platz

Winthir-platz

Str.

Rotkreuz-pl

Nymphenburger

Ⓤ

M

Hirschgarten

Wendl- Dietrich-

str.

NEUHAUSEN

Blutenburg-

Mailingerst

Wilhelm-Hale-Str.

Scharinger Platz

Arnulfstr.

Possart-Platz

Marsstr.

Marsplatz

Ci
K

Ⓢ Laim

Arnulf-

Friedenheimer Brücke

Donnersberger brücke

Donnersberger Brücke

Ⓢ

Ⓢ

Landsberger Str.

Eisenheimer-

Landsberger

str.

LAIM

Fröbel-

str.

Barthstr.

SCHWANTHALER-HÖHE

str.

Agnes- Bernauer-

Str.

Lautensack-Str.

WESTEND

Westend-

Ⓢ St. P

Laimer Platz

Hogen-bergpl.

Ⓤ

Zschokke-

Ⓤ

Ridler

Goller-

str.

str.

Gollierplatz

str.

Gollier-

Schwanthaler-

str.

str.

str.

Schwanthaler-höhe

Theresienhöhe

Laimer Platz

Gotthardstr.

Friedenheimer

Hansa-

str.

Tübinger

str.

Messegelände

Ⓤ

Heimeran-Bayernhalle

71

FRIEDEN-HEIM

Friedenheimer

Str.

H. Thoma str.

str.

Ⓢ Ⓤ

Heimeran-platz

Ganghofer-

str.

Kongreß-zentrum

Theresie

Viebig-platz

Droste-Hülshoff-Str.

Pfaffenhofer Platz

Weißenfelder-platz

Gartenanlage Land in Sonne

Hansa-

Messegelände

Matthias Psch

Bavaria Ruhmes-halle

Fürstenrieder

Stegernburger Str.

Westendstr.

St.-Philippus

park

str.

Ⓢ

(Festwiese)

H.-Fischer- Bavari

Pfronte ner Pl.

Garmischer

Rudi-Sedl-mayer-Halle

Ⓤ

Westpark

str.

SENDLING

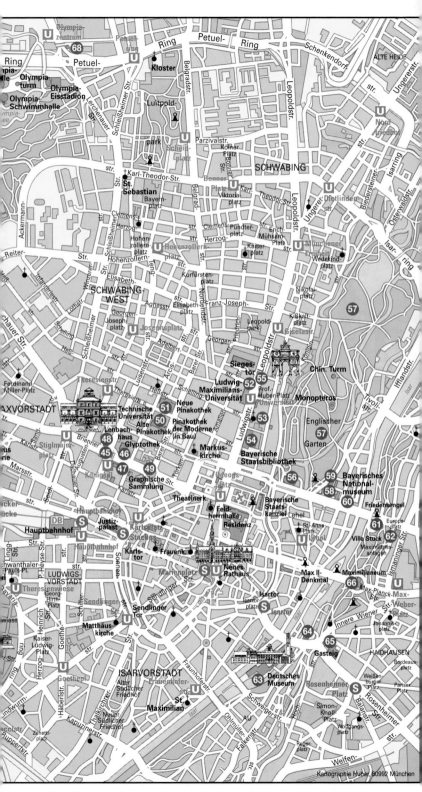